• HALSGROVE DISCOVER SERIES ➤

SECRET DURHAM

• HALSGROVE DISCOVER SERIES ➤

SECRET DURHAM

Photographs and text: PHILIP NIXON

Illustrations: SOPHY NIXON

HALSGROVE

First published in Great Britain in 2016

British Library Cataloguing-in-Publication Data
A CIP record for this title is available from the British Library

ISBN 978 0 85704 290 3

HALSGROVE
Halsgrove House,
Ryelands Industrial Estate,
Bagley Road, Wellington, Somerset TA21 9PZ
Tel: 01823 653777   Fax: 01823 216796
email: sales@halsgrove.com

Part of the Halsgrove group of companies
Information on all Halsgrove titles is available at: www.halsgrove.com

Printed and bound in China by Everbest Printing Investment Ltd

Contents

This book is dedicated to our Labrador, Archie
who was a great friend and companion for
nearly fourteen happy years

Acknowledgements:

Simon Butler and the team from Halsgrove. The staff of Durham Castle.
And our own team: Val Nixon, Mark Nixon and Denis Dunlop.
And Claude...

Site Locations

Key to sites:

1 Durham Castle
2 Durham Cathedral
3 Cathedral Exterior
  and the Bailey
4 The River Banks
5 Church Street Crossroads
6 Durham Market Place
7 Old Elvet and Old
  Durham Gardens
8 Gilesgate
9 Old Kepier and the Wood
10 Northern end of the City
11 Brancepeth
12 Beaurepaire
12a Langley Hall
12b Finchale Priory
12c Ludworth Tower
12d St Laurence Church
13 Croxdale Estate

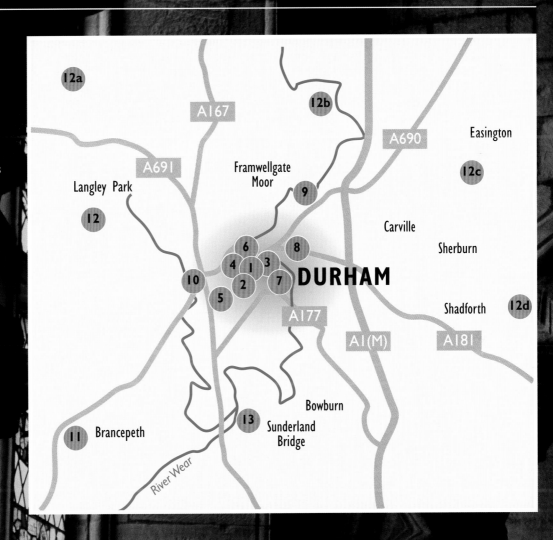

Exploring the Secrets

HALF THE FUN of a book like this searching out the Secrets of Durham and recording that you have seen them. Durham is, by modern standards a fairly compact city, most of which can be explored on foot. Below is a list of the subjects, arranged in groups so that several can be explored in either a half or a full day – depending on how closely you examine what you find. However the last three groups would be better explored by car. A check list is included to mark off those visited.

Durham Castle: The Norman Chapel in Durham Castle is a gem and thought by some historians to be the oldest building in Durham. Best visited by taking one of the excellent guided tours.

Durham Cathedral: Bishop Hatfield's Tomb, Bishop Beaumont's hidden tomb, The black line that marked the area into which ladies weren't allowed, the Bread Oven, the Monks Prisons, and the Galilee Chapel are all to be found in this remarkable building.

Cathedral Exterior and the Bailey: The story of St Cuthbert's Mist, The Cathedral War Memorials, John Meade Falkner, John Gully and the Stink Pipe are all located in the area around the outside of the Cathedral, and its adjoining streets.

The River Banks: Several sites of interest are situated around these wooded footpaths: The Watergate, Prebends' Bridge, The Banksman's Cottage, St Cuthbert's Well, the Galilee Well , St Mary's Well, The Old City Walls and Shipperdson's Cottage.

Church Street Crossroads: The three sites that can be seen here are, Cry for Justice and Wilmore Sculptures – around the University Library, and just beside the crossroads, Charley Cross.

In and Around Durham Market Place: Wickwayne the Usurper (St Nicholas' Church) The Londonderry Statue, The Little Count, and John Duck are all connected within this area.

Old Elvet and Old Durham Gardens: Hangings in Durham (the Prison), Elvet railway, Maiden Castle, Old Durham Gardens, Drummer Boy's Hole are all within walking distance.

Gilesgate: This old area of the City is rich in secrets; The Silver Link Bridge, Vane Tempest Hall , St Giles' Church, The Gilesgate Horse Trough and St Mary Magdalene's Chapel.

Old Kepier and the Wood: Now an area of peaceful country walks but there was once a hive of industry here: Kepier Hospital, Kepier Brick Kiln, The Old Shooting Range, Kepier Quarries and Kepier Viaduct.

Northern end of the city: Several sites can be seen here although they are a little more spaced: North road Drinking Fountain, The Old Workhouse, The Observatory and the Battle of Neville's Cross site.

Brancepeth Village: An attractive village only a short drive from the city: Brancepeth Castle and St Brandon's Church are the attractions here.

Around the Outskirts of Durham City: An interesting and pleasant drive on quiet roads will take in the following: Beaurepaire, Langley Hall, Finchale Priory, Ludworth Tower and St Laurence Church.

The Croxdale Estate: Following the excellent easy footpath through the state will reveal the following: Sunderland Bridge, Croxdale Hall and, Croxdale Norman Church.

CHECK LIST

Hangings in Durham ❑
Elvet Railway ❑
Maiden Castle ❑
Old Durham Gardens ❑
Drummer Boy's Hole ❑

The Silver Link Bridge ❑
Vane Tempest Hall ❑
St Giles' Church ❑
The Gilesgate Horse Trough ❑
St Mary Magdalene's Chapel ❑

Kepier Hospital ❑
Kepier Brick Kiln ❑
The Old Shooting Range ❑
Kepier Quarries ❑
Kepier Viaduct ❑

North Road Drinking Fountain ❑
The Old Workhouse ❑
The Observatory ❑
The Battle of Neville's Cross site ❑

Brancepeth Castle ❑
St Brandon's Church ❑

Beaurepaire ❑
Langley Hall ❑
Finchale Priory ❑
Ludworth Tower ❑
St Laurence Church ❑

Sunderland Bridge ❑
Croxdale Hall ❑
Croxdale Norman Church ❑

Introduction

THE HISTORIC CITY centre of Durham hasn't changed much over the past 200 years. It is the peninsula on which the Cathedral, Palace Green, former administrative buildings for the Palatine and Durham Castle proudly stand, and indeed part of this was designated a World Heritage Site by Unesco in 1986. The act of building on the peninsula was a strategic defensive decision by the city's founders and accentuates the striking position of the Cathedral.

It impressed Symeon of Durham, the historian-monk, so much that he was moved to write in his *History of the Church of Durham*:

> *"To see Durham is to see the English Zion and by doing so one may save oneself a trip to Jerusalem"*

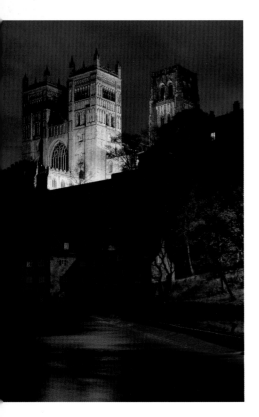

Sir Walter Scott was so inspired by the view of the Cathedral from South Street that he wrote "Harold the Dauntless", an epic poem about the Saxons and Vikings set in County Durham and published on 30 January 1817. The following lines from the poem are carved into a stone tablet on Prebends' Bridge:

> *Grey towers of Durham!...*
> *Yet well I love thy mixed and massive piles,*
> *Half church of God, half castle 'gainst the Scot,*
> *And long to roam those venerable aisles,*
> *With records stored of deeds long since forgot.*

Living in a city of such splendour could possibly breed a sense of complacency, but with Durham, it doesn't. The splendour of this magnificent city drives an urge to find out more, and to discover hidden stories. These intertwine and relate to each other and in the end provide the foundation to our wonderful heritage.

Secret Durham is a project we have been thinking about for a long time and it has given us the opportunity to combine our talents to present what perhaps are the lesser known sites and stories about Durham. Of course one of the deciding factors about which subjects to cover is that the "secret" must be visible. It's not so bad visiting a secret spot if there is something to see, much less interesting if you have to conjure the whole thing up entirely in the imagination.

Our hope is that you will be able to use this book not only as a source of information and a guide, but also as a tick list as you progress around the sites. Most of these places are accessible in a day and several are near each other and quite a few are interlinked through their stories.

Durham is a wonderful city, steeped in history and alive with vibrant visual stimulation – it has been a great privilege to be offered the opportunity to share this with a wider audience.

Sophy Nixon
Philip Nixon
2016

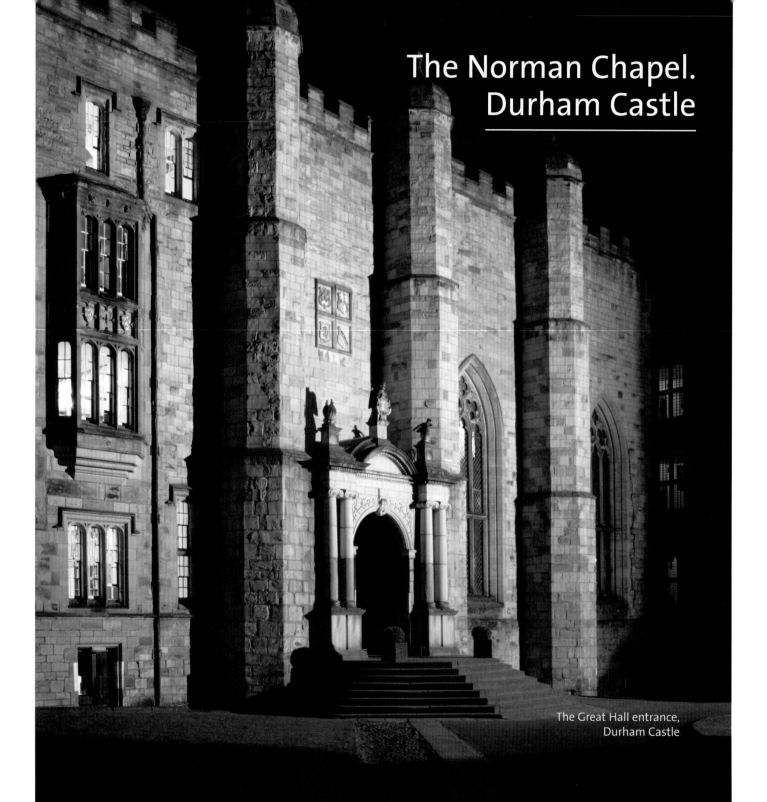

The Norman Chapel.
Durham Castle

The Great Hall entrance,
Durham Castle

DURHAM CASTLE HAS enjoyed a long history of continuous use, and is now home to the students of University College – it is probably the best University College in the world. The castle was originally built in the 11th century as a projection of the Norman king's power in the north of England, because the population in this part of the world remained wild and dangerous even after the upheaval of the Norman Conquest in 1066.

It is an excellent example of the early motte and bailey castles favoured by the Normans. The holder of the office of the Bishop of Durham was appointed by the King to exercise royal authority on his behalf, thus the principle of the Prince Bishops of Durham was established. It remained the Palace for the bishops of Durham until they made Auckland Castle their primary residence and Durham Castle was given to the newly founded University and made into a college.

William Walcher became the first of the Prince Bishops of Durham, a title that was to remain in force until the middle of the 19th century. There is considerable debate about whether or not Durham Castle was originally a stone or a wooden structure. Historic sources mention that its original keep was built of wood, but there is enough archaeological evidence to indicate that even when it was first built it had numerous stone buildings.

The Castle has many wonderful features, such as the Long Gallery, the Black Staircase and the Norman Arch, and the Great Hall; however the college does make extensive use of its two chapels: Tunstall's Chapel, built in 1540, and the beautiful Norman Chapel, which dates from about 1078.

The Norman Chapel is the oldest accessible part of the castle; it has been built with a local stone, which is strongly veined and marked with quite brilliant colouring. The chapel is rectangular in shape, just over 30 feet long, and about 24 feet wide; its overall height is just under 16 feet. It is divided into a nave and two aisles by arcades of four bays. The vaulting is supported by three round pillars on each side of the nave.

In the 15th century, its three windows were all but blocked up because of the expanded keep and thus fell into disuse until 1841 when it was used as a corridor through which to access the keep. During the Second World War, it was used as a command and observation post for the Royal Air Force when its original use was rediscovered. It was re-consecrated shortly after the war and is still used for weekly services by the college. The Chapel is among Durham Castle's most important spaces and is possibly the city's oldest building.

It features an unusual array of carvings, some thought to depict religious scenes and values, others being simply decorative.

One of its capitals depicts a man with two dogs hunting a stag. It is thought that this is a representation of St Eustace, who is said to have converted to Christianity when he saw an apparition of Jesus appear between the horns of a stag he was hunting. Eustace subsequently faced many misfortunes but clung on to his faith. He and his family were later killed by the Emperor Hadrian for refusing to make pagan sacrifices and he became the patron saint of anybody facing adversity. There is also a representation of a mermaid (which symbolised temptation) and of two leopards.

Column capital detail
in the Norman Chapel

The chapel has survived remarkably well for a building of its age. Perhaps the most surprising thing about it is that it has survived practically intact – very important religious spaces like this were often "renovated" to reflect changes in fashion.

Usually access to the castle for the public is restricted to guided tours, but these are well worth booking, to enjoy the secrets of this remarkable building, in the company of an expert guide.

Bishop Hatfield's Tomb

IN DURHAM CATHEDRAL, on the right hand side of the western end of the Quire is the Bishop's Throne or Cathedra, from which the word cathedral derives. The Bishop of Durham occupies this seat on his first visit to the cathedral but on subsequent visits sits near the chancel screen.

It was Thomas Hatfield (1310–81) who built the Bishop's throne in Durham Cathedral, together with a small chapel below. The wall paintings, just visible on the inside, to the left of the Bishop's tomb, are quite remarkable and were probably completed sometime around the mid 1350s. The tomb is a wonderful intricate construction of panels, niches, tracery and canopies, looking as if it has been gently squeezed into the space between two Norman pillars. The structure was restored to its former glory in the early 20th century and looks very striking in its vibrant colours and splendid gilding. It is adorned with a profusion of heraldic shields – notably Hatfield's chevron between three lions rampant, together with a neat carving of the head of Edward III on the front of the stair rail leading to the *"Bishopp's seate"* and the gallery where there are seats for two chaplains on either side of the Bishop. Above his own chair an ornate, rich canopy rises – representing not only his spiritual eminence but also his secular dignity as head of the Palatinate.

Hatfield rose from origins amongst the Yorkshire gentry to become a valued royal servant under King Edward III. As such he took part in the elaborate administration needed to organise the wars France in the late 1330s. Clerical careers in royal administration sometimes led to ecclesiastical office by patronage of the king, and Hatfield's qualities marked him out for early promotion. He became one of the longest serving Prince Bishops, and held office from 1345 until his death 1381. He proved to be an outstanding bishop, instigating major programmes of building, maintenance and improvement. According to a contemporary Durham monk, William of Chambre, Hatfield was also "jealous to excess of any infringement on the privileges of the Church". Given his reputation for pride and haughtiness, it is not surprising, then, that his elaborate tomb is surmounted by his throne, which is famously the highest in Christendom – higher even than the Pope's in Rome. A well-known Durham anecdote

Carving of the head of Edward III – Hatfield's Tomb

Bishop Thomas Hatfield's
Tomb, Durham Cathedral

tells of how, during the construction of the tomb and throne, he allegedly sent two men to Rome to measure the height of the Pope's throne (perhaps one to hold each end of the tape measure?). They returned with the noted information and the Bishop ordered his throne to be made two inches higher – ensuring that if the Pope wanted to sit higher that the Prince Bishop of Durham he would have to sit on a cushion!

As bishop, Hatfield retained a strong connection with royal service and helped manage northern England and England's relations with Scotland. At the same time, he remained a dedicated advocate of the autonomy of the Durham Palatinate over which he ruled as bishop. Hatfield's long episcopacy ensured that he made his mark on his bishopric and on the Cathedral Church of Durham. Hatfield College, Durham University, is named in his honour.

Prince Bishop Lewis Beaumont

LEWIS DE BEAUMONT was nominated as Bishop of Durham on 9 February 1317, thanks to the efforts of his sister, Isabella de Vesci and her close friend Queen Isabella, and was consecrated on 26 March 1318. He died on 24 September 1333.

Just in front of the steps of the High Altar, hidden by a large Durham carpet, is the matrix of a large tomb. This massive slab – about 16 feet by 10 feet – was prepared on the instruction of Prince Bishop Lewis Beaumont in readiness for his death. Unfortunately it has been robbed of its large brass, the magnificence of which we can only imagine; and in spite of all the grand plans and the eloquent words of scripture adorning its edges it only seems to illustrate the complete unworthiness of Beaumont to sit on the Episcopal throne of Durham. Even before his consecration he was a burden to the Cathedral:

The bishopric fell vacant after the death of Richard de Kellowe when Queen Isabella, consort of Edward II, was determined that her close friend's cousin Lewis de Beaumont, should succeed. She wrote to all the monks to advocate his cause and everything was done to help him attain the office. His brother, Sir Henry Beaumont was in the cathedral with a string of retainers during the voting to see fair play – it is said that some of the nobles threatened that if a monk was elected they would cut off his head! The monks, who quite patently didn't care, elected Henry de Stamford of Finchale – but the Queen went down on bended knee to beg the appointment for her cousin – to the point that it was agreed a very large sum of money should be paid into the Papal court. It took the new Bishop 14 years to complete the payments.

The problems didn't end there. On his way north to take up his new position Beaumont's entourage was waylaid at Rushyford by Sir Gilbert de Middleton and his band of "ruffians", who were opposed to his appointment. Sir Gilbert and his men relieved the party of their wealth and sent the accompanying cardinals on their way to Durham but Beaumont and his brother were taken prisoner. Beaumont was sent to Mitford Castle and held for substantial ransom. The prior was obliged to sell habits, jewels and church plate to raise the money. The bishop was consecrated on 26th March 1318 and for the next fifteen years the monastery and the diocese regretted ever having ransomed him – with unparalleled dedication he tyrannised those in the monastery who had opposed him.

Although Beaumont was well born and *"well favoured in countenance"* he was negligent in running the Palatinate, he was unable to lead troops because he was *"lame of his feet"*, and indeed had few other abilities. He had a childish love for collecting and an urge to spend large sums of money – especially the monastery's which he took without a word of thanks: *"he took everything with an affected air of supercilious negligence"*. His education was also lacking for his post – he could neither read nor speak Latin, a serious shortcoming as the papal bull he read at his consecration had to be publicly declared in Latin. In spite of several days coaching he failed miserably – having to resort facetious humour to cover his inability, exclaiming *"By Saint Lewis, he was no gentleman who wrote these words"*. An inscription recalls in extreme generosity that he was considered *"sumptuous"*, perhaps illustrated by an amusing account of how he would entertain his guests with his two pet monkeys. At first one would be chained to his chair and the other would be allowed to move around the dining table feeding greedily on almonds; the restrained one would then be released , thereby setting the two monkeys to fight over the almonds, which they did *"with great screeching"*.

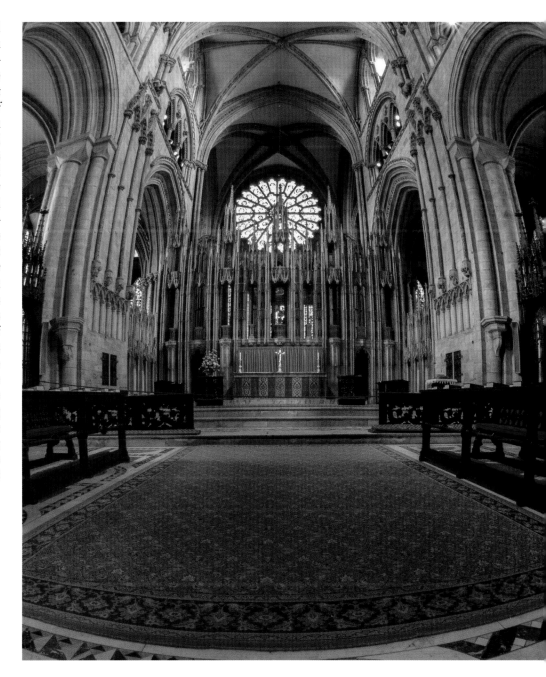

Ladies in the Cathedral

BETWEEN THE NORTH and south doors of Durham Cathedral, at the western end of the Church is a line of black Frosterley Marble set into the floor. The village of Frosterley lies in Weardale about 18 miles to the west of the city. The marble, which takes its name from the village, is really a black Carboniferous limestone containing fossil corals; when it is sawn and polished the result is a beautiful ornate black stone with white fossils, a much sought after decorative building material, used extensively in the Cathedral, and indeed can be found in churches throughout England

This line allegedly marked the point beyond which women were not allowed to pass because of the superstition that St Cuthbert did not like women. One story tells of how the maidservant of Queen Matilda of Scotland hid in the church in defiance of the ban – she was found, almost terrified to death, and then severely chastised by the sacristan, and shortly afterwards became a nun at Elstow in Bedford. The rule was so strict against women entering the cathedral that in 1333 when Queen Philippa, the young wife of Edward III, crossed the line on the way to find her husband's sleeping quarters in the Prior's Lodge, she was forced to find other sleeping arrangements. The Durham monks told the king of St Cuthbert's dislike of women and insisted that she found sleeping accommodation in the castle to avoid upsetting the Saint. The legend could, of course, be just a vicious rumour set about by the French because during his lifetime Cuthbert does not seem to have suffered undue aversion to women: Hilda, Aefled, Ebba and Verca and many other abbesses were his close friends and he even went so far as to found a nunnery in Carlisle. It seems that women just weren't welcome in a Benedictine Monastery and the monks used the power of St Cuthbert to make sure they stayed outside.

Cathedral "Bread Oven"

THE SQUARE-SHAPED recess at the bottom of the wall to the right of the entrance to the tower once contained a fire-place. It was here that the sacrist made the altar bread by pressing dough between the "obley" or baking irons. At other times the fire would be kept burning for heating the warming pans for the priests to warm their hands and the water for washing the altars or the washing of feet on special occasions such as Maundy Thursday.

Paintings in the Galilee Chapel

THE GALILEE CHAPEL, intended for use by women, was built by Bishop Hugh le Puiset between 1170 and 1175. Puiset originally began building at the east end of the Cathedral, adjoining St Cuthbert's feretory, but huge cracks appeared in the stonework and this was taken as a sign of disapproval from St Cuthbert, who allegedly didn't like women, so the work was moved to the west end, overlooking the precipitous drop to the river. The name of the Galilee Chapel alludes to Christ's journey from Galilee to Jerusalem for the events leading up to his crucifixion, a journey symbolised by the monks gathering there before re-entering the cathedral for the mass. The Galilee Chapel is one of the few places in Durham Cathedral where murals with figural representation can still be seen. Much of the Cathedral would have been painted in this way – but the building was whitewashed during the Reformation, and when the whitewash was removed during the Victorian era most of the murals were inadvertently scraped off in the "restoration".

The Galilee Chapel wall paintings

The Galilee Chapel,
Durham Cathedral

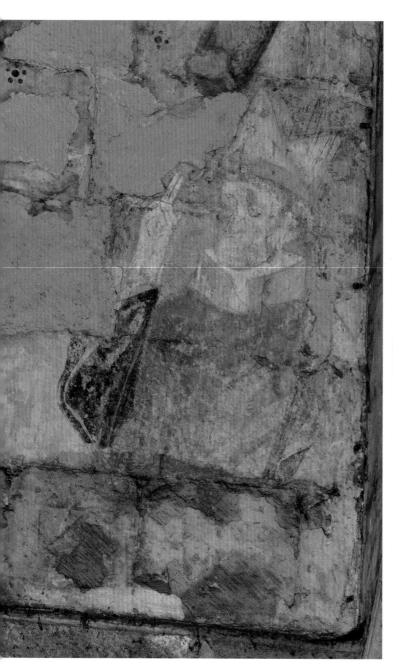

Left: Wall painting of St Cuthbert above Our Lady of Pity Altar, Galilee Chapel
Above: Artist's reconstruction of the wall painting of St Cuthbert

In the north recess of the altar to "our Lady of Pity" there are the remnants of wall paintings contemporary with the building of the chapel; on one side there is what is thought to be the figure of St Cuthbert; and opposite the figure of St Oswald, King of Northumbria. St Cuthbert is seen here, possibly re-invented, wearing the regalia of a 12th century bishop. This new image was probably more easily related to, understood, and recognised by pilgrims to Durham in the late 12th century. This was a crucial time for the church in Durham – Thomas Becket had just been murdered and was quickly building a cult following rivalling that of St Cuthbert. A reinvention of the image of St Cuthbert was embarked upon by Bishop Hugh de Puiset and his followers to slow the decline in the number of visitors to St Cuthbert's tomb.

Below, left: Wall painting and a reconstruction believed to be St Oswald, Galilee Chapel.
Right: Wall painting - Galilee Chapel, believed by some historians to be of St Cuthbert.

The Galilee Chapel,
Durham Cathedral

Centrally, above the altar, although very faint, is a painting of the coronation of the Virgin with Thomas next to James, and again the outline of a figure, thought to be St Cuthbert, can be seen. The soffit over the arch and in the recess is a pattern of a leaf in a heart-shaped medallion – traditionally seen in 12th century manuscripts. The poignant paintings on the arcade show the Crucifixion, flanked by scenes of the 12 Apostles, although sadly the three most western are no longer to be seen. To the left of the Crucifixion is the crucifixion of St Peter and on the other side of Christ, St Paul being beheaded, the crucifixion of St Andrew and the flaying of St Bartholomew. On the other side of St Peter St John is being boiled in oil and St James is being beheaded. Just below two Benedictines monks can be seen praying. To the left of the altar an interesting stone

Left: Possible Green Man carved above the tomb of Bishop Langley, Galilee Chapel

Below: Stone receptacle for offerings, Galilee Chapel

box to accept offerings can still be see, as can the points where the door was hinged, a small aperture to accept coins and a bigger aperture on the top to accept more substantial gifts.

By the time of Cardinal Langley – Bishop from 1406 to 1437 – the Galilee Chapel was almost in ruins. Langley re-roofed it, added stone shafts to each of the Purbeck marble pillars, and prevented it slipping into the river Wear by strengthening the foundations with huge buttresses on the outside. Originally the Chapel was entered through the Great West Door, however, this entrance was blocked up by Langley who made a chantry for himself in front of it, and constructed two new doors into the Nave, one to the north and one to the south. Langleys tomb has a magnificent painted reardos – a representation of the Crucifixion thought by some historians to be by the 16th century Flemish painter Benaert van Orley *"Devised and furnished with most heavenly pictures... lively in colours and gilting"*. But, whoever the artist, it is a captivating addition. Interestingly, above the North Door is a curved stone decoration of leaves with a small circular central relief panel with a carving of what some cathedral experts believe to be the head of a Green Man.

The Monks' Prisons

ON THE SOUTH side of the Chapter House a door leads down into a part of the earliest buildings. These three small, dark rooms were the prison for the monks, where short term sentences were served. No sooner was the sentence passed in the Chapter House than the poor unfortunate who had been caught asleep during psalms or prayers – or whatever his crime – was led through the door to receive his punishment. Of the three rooms one was a chapel, one was for use by a warder, with a small hole in the wall to pass through the meagre rations, and the third was the cell, eight feet square with a 6 feet high vaulted ceiling, a latrine the width of the wall, and a heavily barred door. The monk would serve his time in complete darkness to better commune his soul with the God of Love in whose name he was imprisoned. For more serious offences such as felony or adultery monks would be chained for a year in the Lyng House, a dark cavern 23 feet below the ground

Mysterious weathering in the image of a screaming monk on the Lyng House exterior wall.

Right: The grate covering the Lyng House.

The Lyng House under
the Cathedral

level of the infirmary – only accessed through a trapdoor by a long rope by the master of the infirmary. It was about 60 feet long by 40 feet wide and was in the basement of the stable block of the infirmary. The chamber is 24 feet 3 inches long and had a barrel vault supported by wall arcades made up of older material, some of the capitals of the shafts being of 12th-century, and others of 13th-century date. The entrance was by a round-headed doorway on the south leading into a vaulted passage carried along that side of the building to the west end. Here a newel staircase with a projecting turret ascends into an upper room on the level of the stable floor, probably the master of the infirmary's chamber. This room was lighted by a round-headed window, now blocked, in the west gable, but with this exception no part of the infirmary remains to be seen. Its site was south of the reredorter and south-west of the dorter range. In it was a room known as the Dead Man's Chamber and adjoining it a chapel dedicated to St. Andrew.

Excavations in 1890 under the monks' garden revealed a passage commencing at a depth of about 30 feet at the north-west corner of the stables and rising with a gradual ascent to the south wall of the Galilee, into which it formerly had access. This passage has a barrel vault and is lighted by three narrow slits with sloped sills in the west wall, which abuts upon the river bank; the east wall is blank.

Below: The Monks' Prison, the Chapter House, Durham Cathedral

Below right: Artist's impression of the interior of the Lyng House

St Cuthbert's Mist

BETWEEN APRIL AND June 1942, Germany launched a series of air attacks against English cities of great historical importance featured in the *Baedeker Guide to Great Britain*. These "Baedeker raids" were carried out as revenge for Royal Air Force bombing attacks against the major German cities, including Berlin. The "Baedeker Blitz" was conducted by the German Luftwaffe between April and June in 1942. The aim of the raids was to bomb the most historic parts of Britain, and to damage the British morale. The Germans planned to bomb Norwich, York, Bath, Exeter, Canterbury and Durham – all historic parts of Britain. They aimed particularly at churches and cathedrals, but their aim was not quite good enough, and they missed most of them.

Karl Baedeker was a highly respected German author who wrote and published travel guides, one which covered Britain. It was Baron Gustav Braun von Sturm, a German propagandist who said "We shall go out and bomb every building in Britain marked with three stars in the Baedeker Guide." The Nazis obviously thought that he knew what he was talking about and consequently based their raids on the more historically cultural but much less strategically important cities.

Depiction of St Cuthbert's Mist – RAF window, Durham Cathedral

Durham Cathedral in a mist rising from the river

Gwen Wilkinson, who lived in South Street, which is set high on the river bank directly opposite the western towers of the cathedral, was on duty as an air raid warden when the sirens wailed their eerie sound across the city. Durham was to be the target of one of these "Baedeker raids". As Gwen stepped out of the house and walked along the street she was greeted by the unforgettable sight of the Cathedral, castle and river banks, bathed in beautiful brilliant silver moonlight. She stood admiring the view for what she dreaded could be the last time – Lord Haw Haw had gloatingly broadcast news of these raids a few nights previously – when a mist began to rise from the river. It soon blotted out the scene swirling up and around the central and two western towers of the cathedral. A dark cloud blotted out the moon and the whole area was transformed, shrouded in a dark, dense mist. Gwen stood, transfixed, she heard enemy planes approaching, they circled overhead and unable to locate their target withdrew. The all-clear sounded and Gwen returned home. As she closed her front door she removed her tin helmet and stood in silence with her head bowed, to thank God for deliverance. She was convinced that Saint Cuthbert had protected his Cathedral, his city and its people. This event was confirmed by the Royal Observer Corps and verified by several reliable witnesses.

Cathedral Towers from
South Street

Cathedral War Memorials

County Durham War Memorial
THE COUNTY DURHAM War Memorial was unveiled in November 1928. It was designed by Professor Charles Herbert Reilly, head of the world famous Liverpool School of Architecture. He was awarded the Royal Gold Medal for Architecture in 1943 and was knighted in 1944. This pillar-style memorial stands underneath the exterior of the Rose Window of the Cathedral on a grassy bank. Its neoclassical style with spiral designs echoes the pillars in the Cathedral. It has a simple inscription: "1914–18" and has no reference to 'the glorious dead' or 'sacrifice' but instead the implements of war, steel helmets, mills bombs, machine gun belts and the regimental badge of the DLI are included in relief carvings. The broad stone steps that once ascended to the monument were removed in 1955 and the imposing iron railings went to help meet the demand for this metal during World War Two.

The Boer War Memorial Cross
The magnificent 27 feet high, 12 ton, Boer War Memorial Cross was unveiled in 1905 by John Lambton, the Earl of Durham, and stands on a mound to the west of the north door of the Cathedral. . It is in remembrance of the 153 officers and men from the 1st, 2nd, 3rd, and 4th Volunteers Battalion who were killed in action or died from wounds or disease during the Boer war of 1899–1902; the regimental badge is carved under the shaft of the cross. It is intricately carved displaying entwined branches of oak, birds and relief depictions of warfare in the late 19th and early 20th centuries. On the plinth is the moving inscription,

TO THE MEMORY OF
THE OFFICERS
NCOs AND MEN
OF
THE DURHAM LIGHT INFANTRY
WHO WERE KILLED IN ACTION
OR DIED OF WOUNDS OR DISEASE
IN THE
SOUTH AFRICAN CAMPAIGN
1899-1902
FAITHFUL UNTO DEATH
ERECTED 1905

World War 1 Memorial, eastern end of Durham Cathedral

Right: World War I Memorial

Below: Detail, DLI badge, World War I Memorial

Left: Boer War Memorial,
Durham Cathedral

Above: Boer War Memorial
(detail)

John Meade Falkner (8 May, 1858–22 July, 1932)

JOHN MEADE FALKNER is, perhaps, best known for his novels, *Moonfleet*, *The Lost Stradivarius and, The Nebuly Coat,* although he also wrote poetry and guide books to Oxfordshire, Bath and Berkshire, as well as a *History of Oxfordshire.*

John Meade Falkner's memorial in the cloisters of Durham Cathedral

IN MEMORIAM
JOHANNIS MEADE FALKNER A M
COLLEGII HERTFORDENSIS
IN OXONIA SOCII HONORARII
CAPITALI DUNELMENSIS
BIBLIOTHECARII HONORARII
ARTIS PALAEOGRAPHICAE
IN UNIVERSITATE DUNELMENSI
LECTORIS
NAT MDCCCLVIII OB MCMXXXII
VIRI SI QUIS ALIUS HUMANI
AMABILIS ERUDITI
QUI SCRIBENDI GRATIA
SERMONIS LEPORE
DOCTRINAE VARIETATE
CORDA OMNIUM SIBI DEVINXIT.
HAVE PIA ANIMA

After his retirement in 1921 as chairman of Armstrong Whitworth & Co., one of the largest armament manufacturers in the world he took up the post of Honorary Reader in Paleography at Durham University, as well as Honorary Librarian to the Dean and Chapter Library of Durham Cathedral. Falkner fell in love with Durham and, although he spent his later years travelling frequently, he called Durham his home, living in the Divinity House (now the University Music School) on Palace Green in front of the cathedral from 1902 until his death. There is a commemorative plaque there, while his monument stands in the south cloister of the cathedral.

Moonfleet is a tale of smuggling, and the adventures surrounding a young orphan, John Trenchard . The book has extremely popular among children worldwide up until the 1970s, mostly for its themes of adventure and gripping storyline. It remains a fascinating story widely read and is still sometimes studied in schools. It has enjoyed something of a recent revival being made into a film for TV.

*The Lost Stradivarius,*written by Falkner in 1895 is a short novel of ghosts and the evil that can be invested in an object, in this case an extremely fine Stradivarius violin. After finding the violin of the title in a hidden compartment in his college rooms, the protagonist, a wealthy young heir, becomes increasingly secretive as well as obsessed by a particular piece of music, which seems to have the power to call up the ghost of its previous owner.

John Meade Falkner's House, Durham

John Meade Falkner's Plaque,
Windy Gap, Durham

The Nebuly Coat, written in 1903, is a novel which tells of the experiences of a young architect, Edward Westray, who is sent to the remote Dorset town of Cullerne to supervise restoration work on Cullerne Minster. He finds himself caught up in Cullerne life, and hears rumours about a mystery surrounding the claim to the title of Lord Blandamer, whose coat of arms in the Minster's great transept window is the Nebuly Coat of the title. When the new Lord Blandamer arrives, promising to pay all the costs of the restoration, Westray suspects that the new lord is not what he seems.

The Stink Pipe

ALMOST AT THE meeting point of the North and South Bailey, not far from the entrance to the Cathedral Garth, is an excellent example of a Victorian "Stink Pipe". A clever invention to utilise sewer gas to provide street lighting, reducing a build-up of pressure in the sewers and avoiding the unpleasant consequences of a massive explosion. This example is not just an interesting variant, it is a triumph of late Victorian engineering and proudly states its name on the side: "Webb's Patent Sewer Gas Destructor". Joseph Edmund Webb of Birmingham, patented his destructor on 2 March 1895. At its top, behind a glass cage, burned a small flame from the city's gas supply. This acted as a chimney, and drew the sewer gas up to the flame, where it was ignited, thus illuminating the street. The real cleverness of Mr Webb's design was the way it regulated the supply of sewer gas. Even if there was an inordinate amount of sewage from all the residents of Durham on a particular day, his device meant there was a constant uniform supply of gas to the light and not varying "gusts". This remarkable invention decreased the likelihood of a massive a build-up of pressure in the sewers and the consequent devastating, messy explosion which would most certainly have followed. It made Mr Webb wealthy enough to open a London office, near to the Bank of England in the heart of the capital.

There is evidence to suggest the Stink Pipe stayed in use up to the Second World War when the blackout made it necessary to put out the flame, releasing foul smells into the area. The pipe retained its cage at the top until late 1952. It was such a well-known landmark that is was allegedly the origin of the popular song *"My Grandmother's Fatha Was a Stink Pipe Lighter"*, often heard in the pubs and around the folk and country clubs in Durham.

The Stink Pipe in daylight, the Bailey, Durham

The Stink Pipe at night

John Gully

JOHN GULLY: BUTCHER, Prize Fighter, Publican, Gambler, MP and Durham Pit Owner. The great Durham coal owners of the last century are usually associated with the landed gentry and aristocracy. However one of the most rich and venturesome, and certainly one of the most colourful, was plain Mr John Gully, son of a humble butcher and at one time a champion prize-fighter of England.

Gully was born at Wick, near Bath, in Gloucester, on 21 August 1773. He was the son of an innkeeper who became a butcher shortly after John's birth. His father moved to Bristol, where young John entered the family business. His father, however, died when he was still in his teens and the business quickly declined, young John caring more for the prize-ring than the shop. The business failed completely and at the age of 21, John Gully found himself in the King's Bench prison for debtors in London

A biographer at this time describes him as being a fine, strong young man, over 6 feet tall with rather an open and ingenuous countenance, an innocent tip-tilted nose and beautiful hands of which he was extremely proud all his life. In prison he had nothing else to do but keep himself in condition with

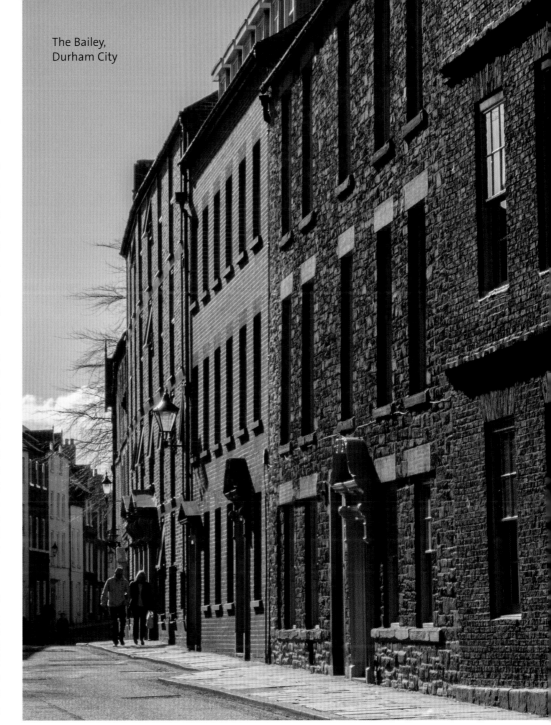

The Bailey,
Durham City

SITE OF HOUSE OF JOHN GULLY M.P. (1783-1863) PRIZE-FIGHTER, RACE-HORSE AND COLLIERY OWNER

the game of "fives", the athletic debtor's one relaxation, and with a pair boxing gloves, which he remarkably still possessed. While in prison Gully was visited by a friend, Henry (Hen.) Pearce, a well-known prize fighter who was nicknamed "The Game Chicken". An informal match was arranged between them in the prison and as a result Gully's debts were subsequently settled. On 8 October 1805, Gully was again matched against Henry Pearce, a fight staged before the Duke of Clarence (later to become King William IV) and numerous other spectators. After fighting twenty eight rounds, which occupied an hour and seventeen minutes, he was beaten. In 1807, he twice fought Bob Gregson, "the Lancashire Giant", for two hundred guineas a match, winning on both occasions. The most eminent prizefighting reporter of the period, Pierce Egan, recorded in *Boxiana* their battle of 14 October 1807:

'Gregson's strength was manifest to his opponent, who endeavoured to ward off its potent effects by his thorough knowledge of the science, and Gulley put in another dreadful facer, which made the claret fly in all directions, when Gregson fell'.

Later Gully became the landlord of the Plough Tavern in Carey Street, London. He retired from the ring in 1808. After a few years as a tavern keeper where he earned the greatest respect, Gully went in for turf speculation. He proved to be such a good judge that in a short time he became quite rich. He bought Hare Park, one of the stateliest homes in Yorkshire, and here some of the greatest in the land were entertained on equal terms by John Gully Esquire. Gully became famous as a spirited breeder and owner. He was appointed Official Betting Agent to HRH The Prince of Wales, later George IV, and he made a great deal of money on betting commissions for various noblemen and gentlemen connected with Newmarket. Gully became the owner of some of the finest racehorses of the day, and the readiness and good humour with which at Doncaster in 1827 he paid out in losses to the tune of £40 000 when Mildred beat his celebrated Mameluke, raised him high among the most honourable members of the turf. His classic successes were the Derby in 1846 and 1854 with Pyrrhus and Andover, the Oaks in 1846 with Mendicant, the St Leger in 1832 with Margrove and the 2000 Guineas in 1854 with Hermit. In 1832 Mr. John Gully was elected to the first Reformed Parliament being returned as Liberal MP for Pontefract. He also represented he same borough in the next election.

Despite his great sporting triumphs, however, Gully is best remembered in County Durham as an enterprising colliery owner and venturesome sinker of new pits. He withdrew from all direct gambling and invested a large proportion of his considerable fortune in the coal development of County Durham. His famous lilac jacket was seen less and less on the turf. The Hetton Company was formed to work coal in the famous Durham Royalty. Gully bought a large number of shares at a comparatively low price. The original speculation was considered be risky since at that time geologists believed that the quantity of coal under the Permian strata was so poor it was hardly worth working. Gully's partners in the venture were Capt. Archibald Cochrane, of Eppleton Hall, a younger brother of the celebrated Lord Edward Cochrane, Mr Baker of Elemore Hall and Mr Nicholas Wood. The latter became manager in 1844. Robert Stephenson was chief engineer of the company. His father George Stephenson was also employed. Thus the partners were in with a chance." We will show 'em whether we cannot make Wallsend coal", said Gully. They got a higher price on the London market than the original Wallsends did. The Hetton venture succeeded beyond the partners' wildest hopes. Gully held on to his shares until they showed a huge profit then he sold out. In 1835 he joined another ambitious speculation, the sinking of the Thornley pits. His chief allies were Sir William Chaytor, Mr Thomas Wood and Mr John Burrell. There was no difficulty in winning the colliery, but labour relations were difficult from the start. Gully was a frequent visitor to the colliery and must have enjoyed the tussles with the colliers and the newly-

Opposite: Plaque marking the site of John Gully's House, the Bailey, Durham City

Below: Artists impression of John Gully as a bare knuckle boxer

formed Miners' Union. He maintained his interest in Thornley until it was sold to a liability company. Again he made a huge profit. Gully also entered partnership with Wood and Burrell in the sinking of Trimdon Colliery, the old pit, and also in the sinking of Trimdon Grange. On 3 January 1861 he paid The Right Hon. John Hobart, Baron Howden, £20 000 for the Wingate Estate and Colliery and remained the sole owner until the day of his death.

Still fit, strong and mentally alert at the age of 78 Gully moved to lovely Cocken Hall on the banks of the River Wear immediately below Finchale Abbey. He was still going racing in 1860, for at that year's 2000 Guineas he met the prizefighter Tom Sayers, fresh from his battle with Heenan. He introduced Sayers to Sir Tatton Sykes, who rose to the occasion. "I shall now go home and sleep sound, for I have shaken hands with the two bravest men in England", he said.

Only in the last few months of his life did Gully's great strength fail him and it was then that he moved into 7 North Bailey, Durham City. He died there at the age of 79 on 3 March 1863. He was buried with great honour at Ackworth Park, Pontefract. The Mayor and Corporation from Durham went to the funeral and carriages of both Yorkshire and Durham drove in the procession to pay their tribute to John Gully Esquire, champion of England. Gully was married twice and had 24 children, 12 to each wife, a truly remarkable man.

John Gully makes a notable appearance in *Royal Flash*, in George MacDonald Fraser's Flashman series of books, and was played by Henry Cooper in the 1975 film version.

John Gully

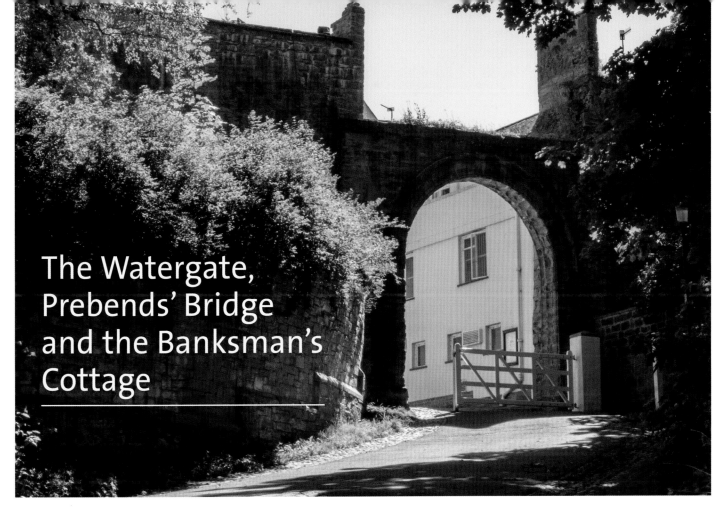

The Watergate, Prebends' Bridge and the Banksman's Cottage

THE WATERGATE MARKS the end of the South Bailey. It was erected in 1778 and replaced the old postern gate in the city wall, which served to guard the river crossing. It was the Reverend Henry Egerton who built this single graceful arch, high enough to allow access by carriages crossing the newly built Prebends' Bridge.

Prebends' Bridge was built in 1777 at the expense of the Prebends or Canons of the Cathedral. It was designed by George Nicholson and replaced the nearby earlier one of 1574 which was washed away in the great Flood of 1771. Prior to 1574 a ferry operated here, and before that there was a ford, to allow pilgrims a route to the cathedral.

This is probably Durham's most 'visited' bridge, thanks to the views it offers of the Cathedral and wooded riverbanks. In fact, when it was constructed it was designed with beautiful views in mind. This was very much the age of Romantic landscapes and the

Prebends' Bridge
in Winter, Durham

exact siting of Prebends' Bridge should be seen as part of an attempt to create a beautiful landscape in Durham. When it was built trees were planted on the riverbanks in order to complete the desired aesthetic effect. In fact this view from the bridge inspired another masterpiece from J.M.W. Turner, and even today this beautiful view continues to attract artists and photographers.

At the western end, an anciently engraved plaque presents writer Sir Walter Scott's thoughts on Durham:

Grey towers of Durham!...
Yet well I love thy mixed and massive piles,
Half church of God, half castle 'gainst the Scot,
And long to roam those venerable aisles,
With records stored of deeds long since forgot.

Prebends'
Bridge in
Autumn

These famous words were composed, we are told, when Scott was one of fifty specially invited guests at a banquet given in honour of the Duke of Wellington by Prince Bishop William van Mildert in the Great Hall in Durham Castle.

Some say he dashed it off on a serviette while he was waiting for his "pudden".

A little further on is the Banksman's Cottage, which has also been known as Prebends' Cottage and Betsy's Cottage. It was probably built at the same time as Prebends' Bridge, in the late 1700s, and served as a dwelling for the banksman employed by the Dean and Chapter to manage the river banks and keep the footpaths free from obstruction. Today it provides picturesque accommodation for University Students.

The Banksman's Cottage,
River Banks, Durham

St Cuthbert's Well, the Galilee Well, and St Mary's Well

UP TO THE beginning of the 16th century the Durham peninsula had, and, indeed still has to some extent, its own natural water supply at a depth of 30 to 40 feet. The castle and cathedral had their own wells, and most of the Bailey houses had theirs. They were, however, also a source of trouble, and in 1540 Bishop Cuthbert Tunstall had a more reliable supply piped to the cathedral and castle from beyond the river.

One of the oldest wells on the Durham peninsula is the Galilee Well and this can be seen just below the Galilee Chapel of Durham Cathedral about half way along the high path from Windy Gap to the ramp leading up to the Dark Entry. The west end of the cathedral is actually built over the well. A metal grill covers a large hole in the pathway, with a stone surround and a very low archway in the cathedral wall, also covered by a substantial grill. The well is today dry and was not known for any particular virtues, but is a notable, although not widely known, example of a Christian building sited over a well.

A short way down the steep banks of the River Wear near the Galilee Well, is St Cuthbert's Well, accessible by a very difficult narrow path, in fact it is probably easier to reach from the riverside path down by the Wear. From the old drinking trough, a hand-railed path leads upwards. Cuthbert's Well has a large sandstone surround with a rounded head-height archway on which an inscription reads 'FONS: CUTHBERT' with a date that could possibly deciphered as either 1600 or 1660. The spring that fed the well emerged from the joint between the underlying shale and sandstone, unfortunately its flow has been irregular since the foundations of the new university library disturbed the rock strata on which it was built.

The less well-known St Mary's Well is located a short distance from Prebends' Bridge by the side of the path leading up to South Street. It consists of an arc of stone walling with a small hollow where

St Cuthbert's Well, below the western end of the Cathedral

water collects. Several 19th century guides refer to this well as being of 'great repute' and 'much resorted to'.

The areas of the city outside the peninsula were supplied by their own wells such as the Framwell, the Southwell, and St Oswald's Well. In 1450 water was brought to the market place from Crook Hall, and a pant or fountain was erected. This continued until 1844, when a water company was formed and the trade of water carrying became a thing of the past. This Durham water company built works outside the south-east corner of the city and pumped filtered river water into a supply reservoir on Mountjoy until 1880. In this year the company was taken over by the Weardale and Shildon Water Company, which afterwards became the Weardale and Consett Company. Thus an excellent supply of beautifully soft, pure water was brought from the wild moorland above Waskerley into Durham City.

Above: St Mary's Well, just below South Street, Durham

Left: The Galilee Well once supplied the Cathedral with fresh water

Durham City Walls

IT IS EASY to overlook that Durham Castle occupied, at one time, much of the peninsula. Massive stone walls were built around the peninsula between 1099–1128 by Bishop Flambard. Although these were most likely developed from earlier Anglo-Saxon defences.

Remains of the Old City Walls, high above the river banks, near Kingsgate Bridge

As well as the wall around the southern part of the peninsula, there was also a wall around Palace Green and eventually another around the Market Place. Those living around the Market Place and the streets leading from it, although subject to Scottish raids, had no protection until after 1312, when Robert the Bruce attacked the city. This disaster led to the building of the wall enclosing the Market Place from the tower on Framwellgate Bridge round the Market Square to the tower on Elvet Bridge, with gates on the northern line of the wall opening on to Clayportgate and Walkergate. This later wall probably didn't have any great military value, but was strong enough to deter raiders..

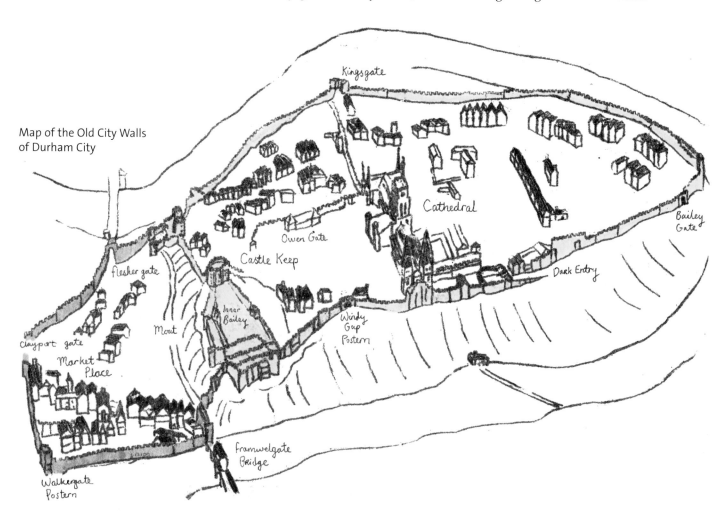

Map of the Old City Walls of Durham City

These walls, strengthened with flanking towers and buttress turrets, followed the contours of the hill rising up from the river banks on all sides except the north, where a wall of great strength, varying from 30 to 50 feet in height, was built to the north of the castle with a dry moat outside this (Moatside Lane).

The massive North Gate, which also served as a prison used to house "lunatics, vagrants and criminals", stood at the southern end of what is now Saddler Street, where it turns into Owengate.

There were two other gates in the walls, leading to fords across the river: Kings Gate which led down to the river along what is now Bow Lane, and the Water Gate or Bailey Gate which stood at the at the southern end of South Bailey.

There was also a postern gate at the Dark Entry in the Priory, and there are also medieval references to a 'Windishole Gate' which could possibly suggest another such gate at the bottom of Windy Gap.

By the end of the 16th century the city walls were badly neglected and allowed to fall into disrepair, consequently large sections of them gradually disappeared.

Remains of the Old City Walls, near the Watergate.

Shipperdson's Cottage or the Count's House

THE LITTLE COUNT'S House, as it is popularly known, stands just south of Prebends' Bridge on a river bend that forms part of the peninsula on which Durham Cathedral and Castle stand. This part of the river is called Count's Corner, and is named after the 3ft 3in Polish dwarf Count Joseph Boruwlaski (1739–1837), who is said to have inhabited this tiny house. Sadly, the Count's House was never Boruwlaski's home. In fact he lived not far away, just up the bank towards the bridge, in a fairly substantial house which unfortunately has now disappeared. It is shown on the 1820 map of the city but after that there is no trace.

Dating from about 1820, this intriguing little building was erected by the Dean and Chapter as a folly, and served as a summerhouse. It is thought to have been designed by Durham architect Ignatius Bonomi and sits gracefully in its lovely riverside setting. The proper name for this charming little building is Shipperdson's Cottage. Named, after Edward Shipperdson, a contemporary of Boruwlaski, who lived at number 9. South Bailey and who was listed among the city's nobility and gentry in the early nineteenth century.

Left and opposite:
Shipperdson's Cottage on Count's Corner, River Wear Durham

Charley Cross, Church Street Head

CHARLEY CROSS IS now sited behind iron railings behind the hedge-line where Church Street curves into Quarry Heads Lane. This rugged stone stump set into a chamfered stone base is all that survives of this 13th century wayside cross – it is thought that it originally stood in the centre of the nearby crossroads. It was moved into the grounds of Bow School but after the war the road needed widening and it was further re-sited in Palmers' Close.

The cross would have served as a monastic boundary stone. Palmers' close was granted to the monastery by Prior Bartram's nephew and was used by pilgrims (or palmers) as a place to tie up (or even graze) their horses while they worshipped at St Cuthbert's shrine. In the early days pilgrims would have descended the deep gorge to cross the river by the ford, but a later wooden footbridge which pre-dated Prebends' Bridge made the journey more comfortable and would allow them to enter the city by the Watergate and walk along the Bailey to the cathedral.

Charley Cross remains,
Quarry Heads Lane, Durham

Cry for Justice - the Scream

CRY FOR JUSTICE – The Scream is the controversial sculpture outside Durham University's Bill Bryson Library. Many students complained that it is a depressing sight.

The sculpture by Fenwick Lawson is based on the iconic Pulitzer Prize-winning photograph of Phan Thi Kim Phúc, taken by Nick Ut, as she was running down a road naked, screaming with pain, near Trang Bang after a South Vietnamese Air Force napalm attack.

However the sculpture is not meant to be depressing, and was not installed to offend. It is in fact a poignant reminder of how students are privileged as members of only one per cent of the world's population who enjoy higher education. It is a sign of encouragement to all refugees and people suffering with the message that one day study and education may help to put an end to such troubles.

This story in particular carries a strong message of hope, in that the photographer rescued the girl and took her to hospital. Even with such slim chances of survival she managed to live through the dreadful trauma and excruciating pain, and was eventually given a home by the photographer. She is still alive today and has set up a peace charity which aims to give help to innocent citizens caught up in war zones.

"Cry for Justice" detail

Left: "Cry for Justice" – Fenwick Lawson

The Wilmore Sculpture

PROFESSOR TOM WILLMORE, a former Head of the Department of Mathematical Sciences and Dean of Sciences at the University, is internationally renowned among mathematicians for his work in the field of differential geometry.

As a result Willmore Surfaces and the Willmore Conjecture have become well known mathematical concepts. Professor Willmore, whose long connection with Durham began with a lectureship in 1946, died in 2005, aged 85, and a postgraduate scholarship fund was set up in his name. In his honour a sculpture of a Willmore Surface was installed outside the Calman Learning Centre on the Durham University Science Site

The granite sculpture, was designed by County Durham-based artist Peter Sales and produced by local firm North East Granite, it depicts a four-lobed Willmore torus – a symmetric Willmore Surface.

Professor Paul Mansfield, Head of the Department of Mathematical Sciences at Durham University explains how the work by Tom Willmore demonstrates both the underlying unity of mathematics and the fact that deep mathematical insights are often inspired by nature. The surfaces named after him arise from a problem in elasticity and yet they have applications in such diverse fields as Einstein's theory of general relativity and cell biology. Studying them led Tom to an important conjecture in geometry which continues to inspire research to this day, both in the thriving pure mathematics group in Durham, which he did so much to establish, and throughout the world.

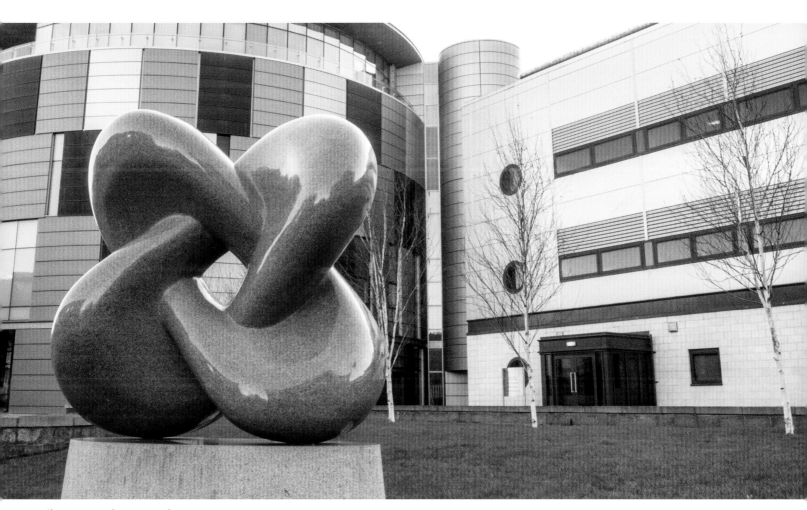

Wilmore Torus by Peter Sales

Wickwayne the Usurper

Pre 18th century drawing of St Nicholas' Church

Right: St Nicholas' Church and the Market Place, Durham

IN 1283, ONLY a few weeks after the death of the then Bishop of Durham, Robert de Insula, the arrogant William Wickwayne, Archbishop of York travelled to Durham to claim, not for the first time, that he had "rights of visitation" there. He attempted to enter the cathedral and was prevented by the monks of Durham. He immediately made his brisk way down to the Market Place, and with the permission of the priest, Galfrid Elemer, he grandly mounted the pulpit and began to excommunicate the Chapter and the new Bishop of Durham, Antony Bek, along with the incumbent monks and placed the entire diocese of Durham under interdict . His glory was short lived, however, when the people of Durham heard of his visit, and why he was here, a

large and very angry group of them gathered outside the church. In abject terror Wickwayne attempted to flee. His fear heightened as the horde was baying for blood and in the tumult one of his horse's ears was cut off. He was saved only when one of the King's commissioners diverted the angry mob and Wickwayne fled down the narrow lane of Walkergate and along the riverside to the comparative safety of Kepier Hospital.

Little is known of Wickwayne's background, as is his place of education, but he was referred to as *"magister"* so he probably attended a university.

The Chapter and Bishop appealed to Rome, and the case dragged on for six years before eventually being settled by a compromise. But Wickwayne died in August 1285 at Pontigny Abbey in Burgundy while on his way to the Papal curia to plead his case against the monks of Durham. He was buried at the Cistercian abbey there in Pontigny, unsuccessful in his endeavour.

St Nicholas' Church Doorway

The Londonderry Statue

The Londonderry Statue prior to refurbishment...

THE STATUE OF Charles William Vane Stewart the 3rd Marquess of Londonderry (1778–1854) is arguably one of the finest equestrian statues in the world. It was sculpted by Rafaelle Monti of Milan and is made from ¼ inch copper plate on plaster. This was the first time this process had been used on such a grand scale. This statue of her distinguished

... and post refurbishment

husband was commissioned by the Marchioness and presented to the city. It commemorates the remarkable life of her husband. He was educated at Eton, and served both in the Old Irish Parliament and at Westminster. He gained a reputation as a brave cavalry officer and served with distinction with the Duke of Wellington in the Peninsular War where he won promotion to the rank of Major General. He was invalided out of the army and raised to the peerage as Baron Stewart of Stewart's Court. He was appointed Britain's ambassador to Austria before moving to County Durham, where he achieved fame as a colliery owner and established the Port of Seaham to export the coal from his mines.

Lady Londonderry was persuaded to pay for the sculpture in advance, Monti claiming that he had incurred considerable financial outlay in its production. Unfortunately, on its completion Monti was declared bankrupt and his creditors seized the statue before it left his workshop. To her dismay Lady Londonderry had to pay a further substantial sum to obtain the statue and her problems were further exacerbated while the substantial plinth for the statue was being erected in the Market Place when several local businessmen filed a court petition claiming its position would interfere with access to the markets, detract from St Nicholas' Church and interfere with their businesses. They wanted it re-sited on the Palace Green. Fortunately the case was rejected and its erection carried out. The statue was unveiled on 2 December 1861 and her life-long friend, the Prime Minister, Benjamin Disraeli spoke most affectionately of his great Friend the 3rd Marquess at the celebratory banquet.

Legend has it that when the statue was finished Monti declared it to be perfect and offered a substantial financial reward to anyone who could find fault. A blind beggar took up the challenge and felt the inside of the horse's mouth with his staff and declared that the horse had no tongue. Monti was devastated. It is said that he was so distraught he committed suicide – however he must have done this very slowly because he didn't actually die until twenty years after the alleged incident, and, of course, the horse does have a tongue. The statue was dismantled, underwent "restoration", and was reinstated in the "new" Market Place at the beginning of 2011.

The Little Count

COUNT JOSEPH BORUWLASKI had great wit, intelligence and personality; he was a talented dancer and musician. He enjoyed the confidences of royalty and nobility, but most remarkably he was a dwarf, never exceeding more than 3 feet 3inches in height. He was born of normal sized parents and claimed that he was normal in every way except size.

Born in Chaliez, Poland, in 1739, only eight inches long at birth, he was one of six children. His elder brother and younger sister were also dwarfs. Sadly his father died when Joseph was only nine years old. His mother couldn't cope and he was adopted by one of her friends. At 15 years of age he became a companion to Countess Humiecka, who called him by a pet name of Jou-Jou, or "plaything", and he was known by this name to many women. She took him to Vienna where he was taught ballet and violin lessons; these talents were ultimately to provide him with a way of making a living.

While he was in Vienna he met the Empress Maria Theresa, who was completely charmed by him when she sat him on her lap. He was given a ring by the six year old Marie Antoinette, the future Queen of France.

On his return to Warsaw Joseph fell in love with a new young French lady-in-waiting, Isalina Borboutin. The Countess tried to break up the romance, to no avail. In spite of threats Joseph left the Countess's house and married Isalina.

Boruwlaski was given a pension of 100 ducats by the Polish king, who it is thought, could possibly have made him a Count. His pension would not support a family – he and his normal sized wife went on to have three children of normal size – and he became a professional entertainer. He travelled far and wide, including the cultural cities of Vienna and Munich. He was well received at the courts of Europe, kings and queens were absolutely charmed by his presence and he achieved great fame and popularity. In Vienna, he met Robert Murray, a British diplomat who encouraged him to visit Britain, where he arrived in 1782.

The Little Count,
Josef Boruwlaski

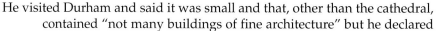

He visited Durham and said it was small and that, other than the cathedral, contained "not many buildings of fine architecture" but he declared that this was "abundantly compensated by the hospitality and kindness of its amiable inhabitants and occasionally by brilliant assemblies, which give us so favourable an opportunity to admire the elegant and beautiful features of the ladies". Ladies were never far from Boruwlaski's thoughts and admiration was often mutual. In a letter to one lady friend, Boruwlaski included a short poem explaining his love for Durham. It read: *"Poland was my cradle, England is my nest; Durham is my quiet place where my weary bones shall rest."*

By the time he eventually retired to Durham in 1791, Boruwlaski had been separated from Isalina for a long time, and was not sorry to hear of her death. He recalled that she constantly humiliated him and recalled with bitterness to friends how she sat him on the mantlepiece during disagreements and treated him like a child.

All his life he went to great trouble to show that he was like any other man and, but he reached old age, he became used to those who saw him as a curiosity. However, his friendship with Stephen Kemble, an enormous, oversized actor and Durham resident, caused much amusement as they talked and strolled the riverbanks together.

His closest friends in Durham were the Ebdon family, of The Bailey, with whom stayed for a time. Just down the riverbank from The Bailey is the so-called Count's House, a folly that was never his home, though he did live in a cottage, now demolished, that stood nearby.

Boruwlaski's Durham days were the quietest of his life, but his memoirs praise Durham and Mr Ebdon.

In his words, Durham was happily adopted to his wishes for a retired life, *"not only from its romantic situation but from being the abode of a friend whose manners were so congenial with my own and whose society afforded me such heartfelt delight"*.

Joseph Boruwlaski died in Durham at 97 years of age. Rarely do dwarfs reach such an age and he eventually qualified for entry in *The Guinness Book of Records*. He was indeed a remarkable man and is buried in the Cathedral under the North Western Tower, his grave marked by a simple slab engraved JB, although his memorial tablet is erected in the nave of St Mary-the-Less, in the South Bailey.

Stephen Kemble – Theatre Manager and actor

DURING THE 19TH century, Durham's new theatre experienced increasing popularity under the influence of a new manager, Stephen Kemble (21 April 1758–5 June 1822).

Kemble had regularly appeared at London's Drury Lane Theatre and was a member of a famous acting and theatre-owning family. He was born in Kington, Herefordshire, the second son of Roger Kemble, brother of Charles Kemble, John Philip Kemble and Sarah Siddons. He married the prominent actress Elizabeth Satchell (1783). His niece was the actress and abolitionist Fanny Kemble. His daughter Francis Kemble married Richard Arkwright junior's son, Captain Robert Arkwright. Kemble's son Henry was also an actor.

Stephen Kemble.

Stephen Kemble became a very successful theatre manager of the eighteenth century English stage. He managed the original Theatre Royal, Newcastle for fifteen years (1791–1806) He was a larger than life actor, famous for performing the part of Falstaff without padding. Contemporary critics acclaimed that in this role Kemble achieved the "optimum balance between comedy and gravity." After his performance in London at Theatre Royal, Drury Lane in 1802, the *Morning Chronicle* wrote: "It is to be regretted that his associations in the country prevent him from accepting a permanent engagement in London." Kemble would return to play Falstaff in London at Covent Garden (1806) and the Drury Lane (1816), for which he received great acclaim. After Kemble's death, the *Edinburgh Literary Journal* wrote, "Kemble was perhaps the best Sir John Falstaff which the British stage ever saw."

Kemble brought actors of a higher calibre to the region and a number of esteemed London performers appeared on the Durham stage. He came to live in the city, and became a popular member of Durham society. He was a close friend of another famous Durham resident, the 3ft 3in tall Polish dwarf, Joseph Boruwlaski. When these two little and large friends strolled along the wooded paths of the city, they must have provided great comic entertainment for the people of Durham.

In later life, Kemble concentrated on theatre management, making only occasional appearances on the stage. His last performance at Durham was in May 1822, a fortnight before his death.

He was fondly remembered by the natives of Durham, and was honoured with a burial in the cathedral.

The heyday of Durham theatre came to an end with Kemble's death, but the theatre continued to operate until 1869, when it was almost completely destroyed by fire.

Stephen Kemble in his most celebrated role – Falstaff

John Duck

JOHN DUCK'S BIRTH and parentage are unknown, but he became one of the wealthiest citizens of Durham. Much of his early life is a mystery but it is known that he arrived in Durham in 1655 where he was eventually apprenticed as a butcher to John Heslop, despite warnings from the Butcher's Guild not to take him on. Initially no one would employ him because he could not, or would not, give any details of his place of birth. At that time this was quite common – there was a resistance to employ anybody who hailed from the Borders – the pillaging and plundering by the infamous Border families had left an abiding fear of anyone who hailed from that part of the world. However it was John Heslop who offered Duck employment; but the Butchers' Guild was up in arms and imposed a hefty fine on Heslop (39s 11d – a considerable sum at the time) for what they considered a gross error.

John Duck was so despondent and remorseful that he made plans to leave Durham and set off dejectedly along the river banks when, to his surprise, a raven dropped a gold coin

Wall plaque marking the site of John Duck's house at the top of Silver Street

Right: The John Duck Memorial , St Margaret's Church, Crossgate

Copy of the woodcut that was once on display above the stairs of John Duck's town house at the top of Silver Street

at his feet, which became the foundation of his fortune. He made his way back to the city and bought two wayward beasts from a farmer driving them to market. He sold the animals at a good profit and in time set up his own butcher's business. He married Heslop's daughter, Anne, and after a few years of successfully investing in property and coal mines his great wealth saw him made Mayor of Durham in 1680 and a baronet seven years later, becoming Sir John Duck of Haswell on the Hill.

He built a large family house at 39 Silver Street, where, at the top of the stairs, a painted panel depicted his story.

He died, aged 69, without issue and was buried in the aisle of St Margaret's Church on 31 August 1691. His wife Anne died in 1695 and was buried alongside Sir John. Upon Duck's death, his fortune passed to his wife's niece, whose granddaughter married the Earl of Strathmore and their son married Mary Eleanor Bowes, whose descendants, the Bowes-Lyons, produced a daughter, Elizabeth, in 1900, the mother of our present Queen.

Hangings in Durham Prison

DURHAM PRISON WAS built in Elvet in 1810, replacing an earlier jail in the Great North Gate across The Bailey, which was causing serious congestion and eventually had to be demolished. Bishop Shute Barrington donated £2000 towards the new building and on 31st July 1809 the foundation stone was laid by Sir Henry Vane-Tempest, Member of Parliament for Durham. After the first architect, Francis Sandys, was dismissed (his work was heavily criticised and deemed unsafe) the celebrated George Moneypenny, leading designer of English prisons, took over the project. Unfortunately Moneypenny died during the construction and the project was finished by Ignatious Bonomi, distinguished Durham architect and surveyor.

The prison had about 600 cells and its first inmates arrived in 1819. Altogether 92 men and three women were hanged at Durham between 1800 and 1958. Ninety one of these executions took place at the prison, or adjacent courthouse – fourteen of them were in public outside the prison, and four were on the public gallows at Dryburn, where North Durham Hospital now stands.

Details on the Courthouse of the window for the prisoner's exit and the holes for the erection of the gallows

Opposite: The Law Courts, Durham

In August 1816 a "new drop" style gallows was erected for each hanging on the steps outside the courthouse. The holes for the beams which supported the platform can still be seen, but are now filled with stone plugs. The condemned person would be led out through a window on to the platform of the gallows above the main door. This was much more secure than leading the prisoner outside to climb steps up to the gallows. Directly opposite the courthouse is a town house with an iron balcony which was rented out to wealthy spectators to watch the hangings. The last public hanging was of Matthew Atkinson for the murder of his wife; unfortunately the rope snapped and the unfortunate Atkinson had to be extracted from under the gallows and a new rope found so he could be hanged again, ten minutes later. Thomas Askern of Yorkshire was never asked to serve in the capacity of hangman in Durham again.

Balcony at Old Elvet used for viewing hangings

After public hangings were abolished by the 1868 Act, a gallows was set up in the condemned prisoners' exercise yard and eventually, about 1890, a purpose-built execution shed was constructed. Durham was one of the few prisons to still have permanent gallows, built in 1925 and housed in a Home Office Execution Block, with two condemned cells.

Mary Anne Cotton, the notorious serial killer, was hanged in Durham on 24 March 1873 – guilty of poisoning three of her four husbands with arsenic, apparently to collect on the insurance policies, although her grand total of murders may well have been as many as 21, including eleven of her own children. It is said she ultimately died not from her neck breaking but by strangulation caused by the rope being cut too short, possibly deliberately.

The last prisoner to be executed at Durham was Private Brian Chandler in 1958, for battering to death 83 year-old Martha Dodd of Darlington, during a robbery.

In common with a lot of prisons Durham allegedly has its own ghost. One night in December 1947 and inmate violently stabbed another to death with a table knife. A few days later another prisoner was locked in the cell. He was found the next morning crouched in a corner overcome with overpowering fear. He told the officers he had witnessed the act of the horrendous murder again and from then no other prisoners would be locked in this cell, and eventually it was used as a store-room.

Elvet Railway Bridge Remains

THE SITE OF DURHAM Elvet Station, near Whinney Hill, was Old Elvet where the magistrates' court is sited today. The area is also the site of student accommodation for the University of Durham. Where the line crossed the River Wear, the abutments of the bridge can still be seen.

Remains of Elvet Railway Bridge crossing the River Wear

Elvet Railway Cottages,
now student
accommodation

The station was opened in 1893 by the North Eastern Railway Co. It was served by a new line branching off the old Shincliffe line at Sherburn House. However the passenger service to Elvet was not a great success and had a short life of less than 40 years and it was withdrawn on 1 January 1931. The station continued to be used for one day a year (except during the war years) until 18 July 1953. That one day was the famous Durham Miners' Gala and on this day special trains were run from most of the surrounding pit villages, bringing miners, their families, bands and banners to the city. The last gala that the station served was on 18 July 1953, and it closed to all traffic on 11 January 1954.

Allegedly, one of the last uses of Elvet Station was in 1953 by a travelling circus that came by train from Europe bringing in all performers which were to appear in the Big Top, presumably pitched on the racecourse. It must have been a memorable and surreal sight: lions, tigers, jugglers and clowns all stepping down on to the platform, and making their way onto the racecourse; an extraordinary occasion.

Remains of Elvet Railway Bridge
at Old Durham, crossing
Old Durham Beck

Maiden Castle – Iron Age Hill Fort

THE IRON AGE Hill Fort in Maiden Castle Wood is one of Durham's enduring secrets, and is likely to remain so until further archaeological work is carried out. It is listed as a scheduled Ancient Monument and there can be little doubt that it was occupied in the Iron Age, and indeed in Roman times, evidenced by their occupation of the Old Durham site, on the opposite bank of the River Wear, a hundred feet below. Such advantageous height would not have been neglected for either defence or signalling purposes. Although the river Wear now touches the site only on one side, the local topography suggests that the position may have been chosen because, at that time, the river enclosed it on three sides, following a course further round the base of the wood, forming a horseshoe almost encircling Hollow Drift, but having since adopted a more easterly course across its floodplain.

The best description is probably given by William Hutchinson in 1823, in his *History and Antiquities of the County of Durham*:

Maiden Castle Durham

On the right and left the steep sides of the mount are covered with a thick forest of oaks: The crown of the mount consists of a level area or plain, forty paces wide on the summit of the scar, in the front or north east side, one hundred and sixty paces long on the left-hand side, and one hundred and seventy paces on the right. The approach is easy on the land side, from the south-west, fortified with a ditch and breast work: The entrance or passage over the ditch is not in the middle, but made to correspond with the natural rise of the outward ground ... The ditch is twelve paces wide, and runs with a little curvature to each edge of the slope, ... on one hand being fifty paces in length, and the other eighty paces. After passing the ditch there is a level parade or platform, twenty paces wide, and then a high earth fence, now nine feet perpendicular ... A breast work has run from the earth fence on each hand along the brink of the hill, to the edge of the cliff or scar. The earth fence closes the whole neck of land, and is in length one hundred paces, forming the south-west side of the area.

Only limited excavation has been carried out on the site, but there is some evidence that the interior of the bank was strengthened with a stone wall and at one time the ditch was crossed by a drawbridge; the excavation unearthed at least one stone bearing a stonemason's mark, which possibly dates the work to the Middle Ages.

The term *Maiden* probably means *a fortification that looks impregnable* or *has never been taken in battle.*

Maiden Castle Durham

Old Durham Gardens, the terrace

Old Durham Gardens

OLD DURHAM WAS first mentioned in the 12th century when it belonged to the rector of St Nicolas' church. By 1268 a chapel and private oratory had been established by the rector Golfrid de Helme.

In 1443, the land owned by St Nicholas', including Old Durham, was given to Kepier Hospital by Bishop Richard Neville, and in 1479 when Ralph Booth was appointed Master of Kepier he, in turn, granted a 99 year lease on Old Durham to his brother, Richard.

In 1545 as part of the Dissolution of the Monasteries the estate of Kepier was sold to John Heath but the Booths continued to live there in the small medieval manor house.

John Heath died in 1591 and is buried in St Giles' Church; he was succeeded by his son John Heath II, who was succeeded in 1618 by his son John Heath III, and it was his brother, Thomas who eventually inherited. In 1630 Thomas Heath sold Kepier to Ralph Cole of Gateshead but retained Old Durham. Old Durham was settled on Thomas's son John Heath IV and his wife Margaret who lived in the North Bailey but moved to Old Durham in 1648. John Heath IV built the mansion and laid out the gardens at Old Durham at some time between 1640 and his death in 1665.

After John's death, the estate was left to his only daughter Elizabeth, and her husband, John Tempest, MP for Durham. The couple continued to live in Old Durham, as did their son William, who was also an MP. In 1719, the Tempests left Old Durham and moved to Sherburn, although the family remained owners of the Old Durham estate until 1794,

The infamous Pineapple Inn,
Old Durham Gardens

and continued to enjoy the gardens at Old Durham. In the ten years between 1725 and 1735 they carried out extensive renovations to the gardens and completely redesigned the gazebo.

The Tempests had left Old Durham by 1748, by which time it was run as a commercial nursery by gardener John Thackray and then by his widow, Jane.

Throughout the 1750s, music concerts were held at Old Durham. The *Newcastle Courant* reported a concert in June 1753 at which the *"Choir of Durham performed a grand Concert of Music to a brilliant Assembly of Gentlemen and Ladies"*. The following May, the newspaper reported a *"concert of vocal and instrumental musick(sic)"*, performed to an audience *"very large and genteel"*, and again the following year a concert was run by the celebrated composer John Garth, famous organist of Durham Cathedral.

By 1776 the upper garden had been enclosed with a high stone wall to allow the cultivation of south facing fruit trees. But documents show that by 1776 the mansion at Old Durham had been demolished and probably sold as building materials. In 1787, William Hutchinson, the renowned Durham historian, described the gardens:

"The gardens are formed into terraces of a considerable length. This sweet retirement has become a place of public resort, where concerts of music have frequently been performed in the summer evenings, and the company regaled with fruit, tea, etc. The gardens are open all summer for rural recreation. The terraces command the elegant valley prospect before described."

In 1834, the Pineapple Inn was already established as a public house supporting the commercial and recreational activities of the gardens. Indeed , a commercial nursery was still operating at Old Durham in 1844. The first edition Ordnance Survey map of 1857 shows the walled gardens as a bowling green. In 1918, Lord Londonderry, descendent of the Tempests, sold the Pineapple Inn and Old Durham Gardens to Victor Mazzini Walton. Mr Walton was an artist and ice cream maker and continued to develop the gardens as a pleasure ground for public recreation. A 1921 advert describes it as having tennis courts, putting green, running track and a tea garden.

But five years later the Pineapple Inn it lost its licence, some say due to its unfavourable reputation - its customers enjoying "lock-ins" and "stoppy backs". However the inn continued to serve soft drinks, including pineapple juice, while the weekend dances were a regular feature of Durham life between the wars. Sadly, after the Second World War the Old Durham dances died out and in 1949 Mr Walton sold the land. The Pineapple Inn became Pineapple House, and the public entrance was blocked up. The gazebo, its walls, terraces and gardens gradually slipped into decline and disrepair.

In 1985, the City of Durham Council bought Old Durham, and began a programme of conservation and restoration. The gazebo was repaired, the terrace and slope were restored, and archaeological excavations carried out and the garden planted to historic layouts. In 1998, English Heritage placed Old Durham on the Register of Historic Parks and Gardens (Grade II).

Drummer Boy's Hole

IN THE LATE 1700s the ford across the River at the eastern end of Pelaw Wood was very dangerous and great care had to be taken when crossing. A story from this time recounts how, on a winter's evening during a particularly murky dusk, a young drummer boy with the Durham Militia missed his footing during crossing and stumbled into a hole in the riverbed and drowned in the icy water, in spite of frantic attempts by his fellows to rescue him. It is said that, at dusk on a winter's evening, when the conditions are right, the sound of drumbeats can be heard as the ghost of the unfortunate boy tries to pick his way over the treacherous ford...

Above: The spooky descent to Drummer Boy's Hole river crossing

Right: Artists impression of Drummer Boy's Hole when the tragedy took place

The supposedly haunted Drummer Boy's Hole river crossing

The Silver Link Bridge

THE SILVER LINK Bridge on the edge of Pelaw Wood was built across Pelaw Beck to commemorate the Silver Jubilee of George V and was opened on 12 April 1938.

It was built by the Cleveland Bridge & Engineering Company of Darlington, at a cost of £805. The elegant design was by Mr J.W. Green, City Surveyor and Engineer, and incorporated some of the features found on the bridge that spans the Zambezi Falls.

A civic party was led over the newly opened bridge by the Mayor, Councillor W.E Bradley and the chairman of the Parks Committee Alderman Dickeson.

This welcome structure provides an easy route from Gilesgate to Pelaw Wood. Prior to this the only way to negotiate this deep ravine was by a precarious steep descent followed by a very stiff climb.

However, locals are still wary about using the bridge at night – it is reputed to be haunted by a grey lady searching for her lost child.

The Silver Link Bridge,
Pelaw Wood

The view to Durham
Cathedral from Pelaw
Wood

Vane Tempest Hall, Gilesgate

THE VANE TEMPEST Hall in Gilesgate is the only surviving example of a militia barracks in County Durham. The Durham Militia was formed in 1759 and Lord Vane, Earl of Darlington was colonel of the regiment. The officers were chosen from among the local gentry while the rank and file were selected by ballot. Britain has had a long history of reliance on part-time soldiers to supplement the standing regular full-time army. These forces were often assembled as needed for defence against invasion, or for maintaining domestic order. These men were not allowed to serve abroad, but there was good financial incentive if they joined the "regulars".

The Militia was the oldest of the auxiliary forces and was first recorded in 1558, but its origins can be traced right back to the 9th century. In 1853 the Durham Militia was divided into the North Durham Militia, based in Gilesgate, and the South Durham Militia , based in Barnard Castle. These two groups formed the 3rd and 4th Battalions of the Durham

Vane Tempest Militia
Barracks, Gilesgate

Light Infantry and fought in the Boer War from 1899 until 1902.

Vane Tempest Hall itself is a hidden gem, just behind the buildings at the junction of Sherburn Road and Sunderland Road. Its imposing facade is best appreciated from the adjacent bowling green. The grand scale of the gothic-style windows with the imposing turret over the entrance is quite remarkable. As a Militia building, it was set in more extensive grounds and the remains of the surrounding walls give some idea of its original size. The former parade ground and other associated buildings that formed the typical courtyard perimeter have been lost over time to new development, but it remains an imposing site, high on the valley side, overlooking Pelaw Wood.

By 1884 the Militia vacated the barracks and it was pressed into service as a hospital for smallpox cases. However in 1893 the building was bought by the Marquess of Londonderry as headquarters for the 2nd Durham Artillery Volunteers. Today the hall serves as a busy community centre, although it is reputed to be haunted by the ghost of a soldier who was executed in the courtyard for mutiny.

Far right: Lookout tower North Durham Militia Barracks

Right: North Durham Militia shako plate

St. Giles Church , Gilesgate

ST GILES CHURCH is a grade I listed parish church and stands, set back from the road, at the top of Gilesgate Bank It was built as the hospital chapel of the Hospital of St Giles and was dedicated in on St Barbara's Day, June 1112 by Bishop Ralph Flambard to "the honour of God and St Giles". The church became caught up in an 1140 dispute over the bishopric of Durham following the usurpation of the diocese by William Cumin, Chancellor of King David I of Scotland. William of St. Barbara, the rightly elected Bishop, was forced to retreat to, and fortify, the church after his entry into Durham was beaten back by Cumin's men. In response Cumin's men destroyed the hospital, which was later re-founded at nearby Kepier.

Bishop Hugh Puiset later extended the church to reflect its role at the centre of a growing parish, and the current font is believed to date from this time. The church was allocated to Kepier Hospital which acted as rector, receiving tithes and with the advowson (right to appoint a vicar), appointing a parochial chaplain to minister to the needs of the parish.

John Heath, the Elizabethan owner of the Kepier estates, Gilesgate and Old Durham is buried in the church.

The ecclesiastical parish of St Giles was divided in 1852 with the creation of a new Belmont parish, served from church of St Mary Magdalene, Belmont and covering Belmont, Gilesgate Moor and New Durham.

St Giles Church retains some of Flambard's original building (primarily the north wall) and most of Puiset's additions. Minor restoration and three large windows were inserted into the south wall in 1828. The church was restored and extended in 1873-1876 as the parish continued to grow.

St Giles Church from the edge of Pelaw Wood

Opposite: St Giles Church, Gilesgate

Saint Giles is the patron saint of cripples and is also invoked as a saint for childhood fears, convulsions, depression. In medieval art, he is depicted with his symbol, the hind. His emblem is also an arrow. According to his early history he withdrew deep into the forest near Nîmes, where in great solitude he spent many years, living on a vegetarian diet. His sole companion was a deer who sustained him on her milk. This retreat was discovered by the king's hunters, who had pursued the hind to its place of refuge. An arrow shot at the deer wounded the saint instead, who afterwards became a patron of cripples. The king, who by legend was Wamba, a wild heathen Frank, developed high esteem for the hermit's humility, and built him a monastery in his hidden valley, Saint-Gilles-du-Gard, which Giles placed under the Benedictine rule. Here he died in the early part of the 8th century, with the highest repute for sanctity and miracles. Giles is one of the Fourteen Holy Helpers, and the only non-martyr, initially invoked as protection against the Black Death. His feast day is 1 September.

Gilesgate Horse Trough

Gilesgate horse trough

Right: The Elvet horse trough

THE TROUGH STANDS at the top of the long, steep Gilesgate bank, on the road between St Giles – reputed to be the second oldest church in Durham – and what is locally referred to as the Duck Pond. While there is no pond visible today the old horse trough still survives to mark its location.

It was moved here in 1896 from Elvet to replace the old one which in turn had been moved to make room for a smart new one presented to the city by Coroner Graham and his wife.

Although it is now used as a planter, in its day it would have provided a drink of cool fresh water for the horses that had pulled their heavy loads up "Gillygat" bank.

Tinklers' Lane

TINKLERS' LANE IS a cobbled "vennel" or passageway which ran steeply from the top of Claypath down to the riverside and formed the boundary between the parishes of St Nicholas and St Giles.

Stumbling over the centuries-old cobbles or sets, between the high whitewashed stone walls that seem to block out the modern world, it is easy to imagine the sound of tinkers repairing pots and pans for the local townspeople. They brought their kitchen utensils here because tinkers were banned from the city streets. It was here that these traders also sold their wares and careful investigation reveals some of the hooks, still visible, on which they hung their pots, pans and utensils for sale.

The original length of lane has been shortened by the Leazes Link Road. It originally emerged right on the riverside path between Baths Bridge and Elvet Bridge. There was a very primitive public urinal positioned near the Claypath entrance, but this too has been removed, although the cobbled surface of the lane survives to confirm the antiquity of this secret lane.

An observation window can be seen high in a gable end at the junction of Gilesgate and Claypath, strategically placed to look out from any invasion from the coast approaching over the top of the hill from Gilesgate, to the east.

Pots and pans were sold
in Tinklers' Lane

St Mary Magdalene's Chapel, Gilesgate

THE ENIGMATIC RUIN of St Mary Magdalene's Chapel in Gilesgate, which once served as a chapel for a small hospital, is said to have been founded by John le Fitz Alisaundre, a Norman nobleman. The establishment had a priest and 13 brethren and sisters who were defined in the ancient deed as *"Men and women who had been well-to-do folks and in good repute in their early life and whose wealth has passed away..."* It further instructed that these people were to be taken into the hospital *"without giving anything for their entry"*. These Maudeleyans, as they were known, were clothed and fed under the jurisdiction of the Almoner of Durham Cathedral. It was stated in the regulations that the Hospital Chaplain had to wear a monk's habit which would be replaced every year; the brethren and sisters received "three ells" of russet canvas for clothes and fourpence for shoes. They were also supplied with 23 loaves of bread a week, supplemented by broth on three days a week. In 1391 Bishop Skirlaw granted an indulgence to all those who supported the hospital.

Because of the soft ground it was built on the chapel eventually became unsafe and ruinous and had to be rebuilt a few yards from its original site in the late 1440s.

The new chapel was consecrated on 16 May 1451 and enjoyed all the rights of a Parish church even though its parish was only 23 acres. After the Dissolution of the Monasteries in 1546 the chapel continued to be used as a place of worship until the end of the 17th century, by which time its fabric had become dangerous and unsafe.

Remains of the north window,
St Mary Magdalene's Chapel, Gilesgate

Opposite: The Chapel of St Mary
Magdalene, Gilesgate

Kepier Hospital (the Hospital of St Giles of Kepier)

KEPIER HOSPITAL, or more correctly, the Hospital of St Giles of Kepier was originally founded at Gilesgate, Durham, by Bishop Ranulf Flambard as an almshouse "for the keeping of the poor who enter the same hospital". It was dedicated to God and St Giles, the patron saint of beggars and cripples. The first hospital chapel (now St Giles Church) was dedicated in June 1112. Other than the church, the original buildings were wooden or wattle-and-daub structures. Flambard endowed the hospital with a range of lands, including the manor of Caldecotes, the mill on Durham's Milburn, and corn from fifteen of his villages. Godric of Finchale was a doorkeeper of the hospital church before settling at Finchale.

Kepier Hospital and Farm

The hospital buildings (with the exception of the church) were destroyed along with Caldecotes by the men of William Cumin, Chancellor of King David I of Scotland, who claimed to be the rightfully elected Bishop of Durham. Cumin took up residence in Durham Castle and for three years arrogantly abused his falsely-claimed powers, persecuting local people with the help of his band of heavily armed ruffians. When, in March 1143, William De St Barbara was elected as the true Bishop of Durham and he marched north with a band of loyal supporters including Roger Conyers.

They fully expected the usurper to stand down. However he wouldn't, and didn't, and furthermore would not allow De St Barbara anywhere near the castle, who had no alternative but to take refuge in St Giles' church. The following morning Cumin and his men broke down the church door and a vicious sword battle broke out between the two bands of men while terrified monks prayed fervently for it to stop and one of them was nearly killed by a huge stone thrown by Cumin's men. De St Barbara admitted defeat and left Durham.

He returned in August 1144 accompanied by the Earl of Northumberland's army and Cumin fled, but not before he had burned the Hospital of St Giles to the ground – he was eventually captured by Roger Conyers at Kirk Merrington.

Kepier Fish Garth remains

The hospital was refounded beside the River Wear at Kepier, in 1153, by Bishop Hugh le Puiset with an establishment of thirteen brethren, serving around thirteen (male) inmates as well as travellers and pilgrims. Puiset bestowed more lands, including the village of Clifton, a lead-mine in Weardale, a peat bog at Newton, and more rights to corn from the Bishop's villages (gillycorn). In order to further secure the finances of the hospital, Puiset also granted a charter allowing the creation of the borough of St Giles, the nucleus of modern Gilesgate, with many burgesses probably drawn from Caldecotes and Clifton.

Kepier was frequently bound up with the politics of the border country, with Edward I and Queen Isabella staying at the hospital in 1298 on their journeys north. Kepier suffered from raids by the Scots, particularly in 1306 by Robert the Bruce and his men who set fire to the buildings during their vicious raids. Much of the hospital had to be rebuilt – the existing gatehouse dates from the 14th century.

Following the Dissolution of the monasteries Kepier passed out of the hands of the church and in 1568 it was bought by a Londoner called John Heath, a close friend of Bernard Gilpin, the "Apostle of the North"

The Heath family, made substantial alterations to the hospital site, including laying out of gardens and the erection of a mansion where the chapel and infirmary may have once stood. By 1827 this house had become a 'Kepier Inn' or the 'White Bear'. Kepier Mill survived until 1870, when it was destroyed by fire. Of the hospital site itself, the gatehouse is intact, the mansion survives as ruins, and the farmhouse is in private use.

Kepier Fish Garth remains

The site is now a Scheduled Monument with grade I and grade II* listed building status. The West Range is included on English Heritage's *Buildings At Risk* register.

The first hospital church remains in use as the parish church of St Giles, Gilesgate. No other buildings from the first hospital survive.

Kepier Brick Kiln

THE BRICK KILN at Kepier is the only remnant of a series that lined the road to Kepier Colliery. It is thought to be of a Scottish design, unusual in this area, as the Newcastle type would normally be expected.

Brick making was recorded as being well established on this site in 1828 when Thomas Jackson, a local builder and stonemason was listed as proprietor. The firm became Thomas Jackson & Son of Claypath in 1848. They were succeeded by Eleanor Jackson in 1848 who was described as a brick maker and stonemason of The Sands, and operated until 1857.

Ralph Dixon took over as the owner of Kepier Colliery in 1857 and by 1860 the brickworks was controlled by John Thwaites. It then passed into the hands of W. Tinker but does not seem to have operated beyond that date.

Opposite: Kepier
Brick Kiln

Looking inside
Kepier Brick Kiln

However after that it became a fascinating magnet for young boys on their way down the "Banky Fields" to sample the apples in Kepier Orchard. Nearby was a large pond, locally called Harpers Pond, that was, allegedly, bottomless and a procession of cows, sheep and even a man and a horse and cart were rumoured to have disappeared into its fathomless depths.

The Old Shooting Range

ALONG THE FOOTPATH beside the river Wear from Kepier Hospital to Kepier Wood, the remains of a shooting range can be seen in the last open field. The two thick concrete bulkhead remnants are all that survive of the rifle range that was allegedly established in the 19th century and first appeared on the second edition Ordnance Survey maps of 1894–1899). The range is shown to extend at least 900 yards from the River Wear, south-west

Remains of the rifle range, Kepier, formerly used by the DLI

towards Kepier Hospital. The 900 yard range is still shown on the fourth edition OS maps but it seems to be shortened to just the first 400 yards on fifth edition maps of the 1950s. At this time there was still quite a substantial building visible, with a corrugated iron and wood shelter towering over the concrete butts. However it seems to have fallen into disuse towards the end of the Second World War. The range was in use during the Great War (1914–1918) and the Second World War (1935–1945), seeing use by both the regular and Territorial Army, and some historians believe there was also a connection associated with the one time Militia barracks at Gilesgate, now the Vane Tempest Community Centre.

The range was a high point on Sunday afternoon dog walks for the author in the late 50s, whose father could remember zeroing rifle sites for soldiers of the DLI , practising on the range in the days just before World War II.

Kepier Quarries

KEPIER'S LONG-ABANDONED quarry faces form a rugged backdrop for the trees which have now naturalised this riverside walk. This area is a little more remote from the popular river banks of the city, but is much appreciated by locals familiar with this stretch of the river.

The quarries range almost continually along the length of the woodland. This immediately prompts the question of where all the stone has been used. It is sandstone and, of course, unlike limestone, can only be used for building; moreover most of the stone-built houses in the area are of limestone.

Some historians believe that Kepier was the source of some of the building stone used for the cathedral; in fact there were stories that with vary careful searching it was possible to find part-finished columns, blocks and other large pieces of carved masonry. There is, of course, evidence of much stone extraction around the peninsula, but quality also plays an important part in the choice of raw materials.

By 1895 most of the quarries were played out, in fact the only one left in use was the one nearest the city. The only way to the quarry was by crossing the line which ran into Gilesgate Station. There is a record of an accident happening here in June 1844.

Mr Jackson, a city mason, was crossing the line when the 9 o'clock train suddenly hit his cart. Sadly both horses died instantly but Mr Jackson miraculously escaped with only a few bruises.

Fortunately a walk through Kepier Wood today is not as risky. The railway closed in 1966 and the quarries stand in silence, reclaimed by nature and transformed into a wonderful riverside haven for, flowers, birds and wildlife with just the odd pixie and goblin frolicking through the woodland glades!

Opposite: Kepier Quarries – Cathedral stone was quarried here

Right: Part of the extensive Kepier Quarries

Belmont
Viaduct

BELMONT VIADUCT WAS one of five built by the North Eastern Railway originally to service the coalfield at Crook. Four of these still stand; two of them have been incorporated into the East Coast main line and one has been converted to a road bridge. The remaining one crosses the River Wear at Belmont, just to the east of Durham City. It remains untouched, standing just as built in 1856. It looks forlorn above the riverside footpath – it has no use. It is fenced off at both ends and there is no footpath across it, nor is there ever likely to be because what remains of the railway it once carried runs out in about 500 meters into the A1(M) motorway.

This magnificent bridge bestrides the gently flowing river with its eight graceful arches, giving it a certain elegance to the wooded gorge. Because it can only be viewed from below its height of 130 feet makes it look very impressive, no doubt as was the desire of the mid 19th century architects and builders, in this case the renowned company of Mr Richard Cail of Newcastle.

Opposite: Belmont Viaduct carried the main Sunderland railway line high over Kepier Wood

Right: Belmont Viaduct reflected in the River Wear.

The North Road Drinking Fountain

IN MID 19TH century London, water provision from private water companies was generally inadequate for the rapidly-growing population and was often contaminated. Legislation in the mid nineteenth century formed the Metropolitan Commission of Sewers, while The Metropolitan Free Drinking Fountain Association was established in 1859. The first fountain was built on Holborn Hill against the railings of the church of St Sepulchre-without-Newgate on Snow Hill, and opened on 21 April 1859. In the next six years 85 fountains were built, with much of the funding coming directly from the Association which soon became associated with the temperance movement since their fountains provided a suitable substitute for alcohol and were often positioned outside public houses.

The North Road drinking fountain in Durham was erected by public subscription on 27 October 1863 and was originally on a site where the railway viaduct crossed North Road at the corner of Atherton Street. The Fountain has now been moved to the base of another pier. It was designed in the Gothic style, using mainly Dunhouse stone further embellished with Peterhead Red Granite columns and a Rubislaw Grey Granite centre panel. The source of the water supply was piped here from the Flass Well and was piped here to two gargoyles, serving first the marble drinking bowl and then passing to the dog trough below. Sadly the fountain no longer functions but serves as an excellent example of a piece of wonderfully designed Victorian street furniture.

Opposite: North Road drinking Fountain

Left: The niche for dogs to drink at the North Road drinking Fountain

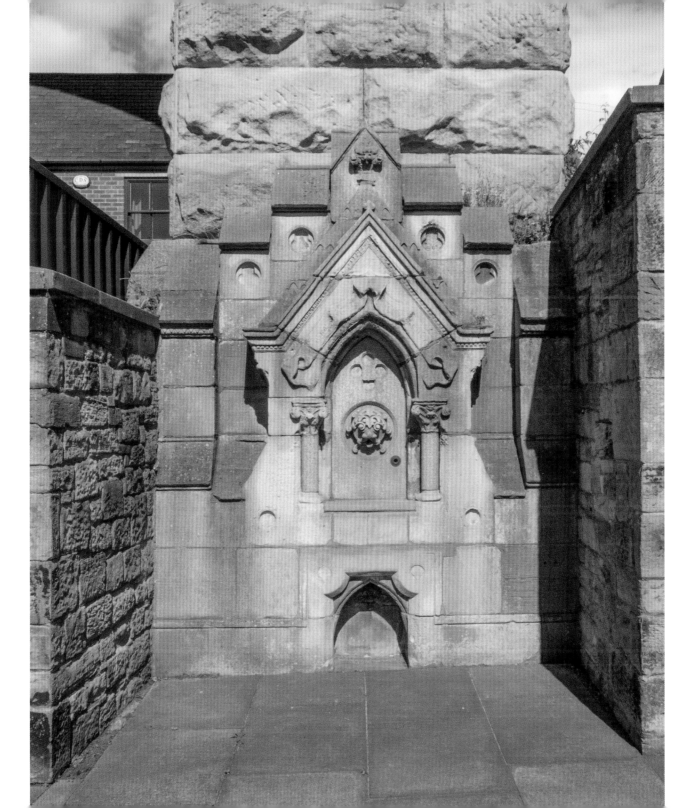

The Old Workhouse

DURHAM UNION WORKHOUSE was built in 1837 on Crossgate by architect George Jackson. It was originally intended to accommodate 150 inmates. Poor infirm people were given food and shelter while the more able bodied were still given shelter but had to work for their keep. In about 1870 an infirmary block and fever wards were added and by 1875 new casual wards and a block for the infirm were built. The workhouse layout comprised an administrative block facing Crossgate with a rear wing linking it to a parallel rear range. This returned towards the street with a rectangular wing at its west end. The layout subsequently altered with the addition of new buildings. By 1895 the rear range had been replaced by an L-shaped range and the west wing had been demolished. In 1857 the workhouse comprised inmates' accommodation, a dining-hall (also used as a chapel), a board room, sick rooms, receiving wards, kitchens, a pantry and school rooms. Between 1870 and 1875 an infirmary and fever wards were added at a cost of nearly £4000. The architect in this case was William Crozier. In 1875 casual and infirm wards were built and, later, additions were carried out to the infirmary and casual wards. In 1891 part of the original building was demolished and a dining hall was erected. In 1894, *The British Medical Journal* set up a commission to investigate conditions in provincial workhouses and their infirmaries. Following a visit to the Durham establishment, the commission's report found much to criticise. The infirmary building, although of comparatively recent construction, did not provide adequate separate accommodation for children or "offensive cases". There were no bathrooms, and the water-closets were badly located. Much of the nursing was carried out by untrained "attendants". The commission recommended the building of a new infirmary, staffed by a full complement of trained nurses.

H.T. Gradon, the architect, designed further additions in 1897 and 1911. A new isolation block was erected in 1915 and the laundry was rebuilt. After 1930 the Workhouse passed from the control of the Guardians to Durham County Council and was renamed Durham Public Assistance Institution. In 1933 a female casual ward was built and the male casual ward renovated. The Institution later became Crossgate Hospital. After the inauguration of the National Health Service in 1948, it became St Margaret's Hospital. The buildings were predominately two-storey stone buildings although some of the later additions were built of brick. Over the last few years the series of building, some parts of which are Grade II listed, have been converted for use as housing, medical and dental surgeries, student accommodation and a care home.

Opposite: The Old Workhouse

Below: Building detail of the Old Workhouse

Durham University Observatory

THE DURHAM UNIVERSITY Observatory is a weather observatory owned and operated by the University of Durham. It is a Grade II listed building located at Potters Bank. The Observatory was founded in 1839 initially as an astronomical and meteorological observatory (owing to the need to calculate refraction from the air temperature) by Temple Chevallier. However in 1937 it moved to purely meteorological recording. The observatory's current Director is Professor Tim Burt of the Geography Department.

After the Radcliffe Observatory, Durham has the longest unbroken meteorological record of any University in the UK, with records dating back to the 1840s, principally due to the work of Gordon Manley in creating a temperature record comparable to that of Oxford University. Today, the observations are made using an automatic weather station; this provides on-line data to the Meteorological Office and allows the observatory to maintain its long records.

Opposite: The Observatory

Below: Durham Cathedral and Durham School from Observatory Hill

The Battle of Neville's Cross

Battle of Neville's Cross
Sculpture - Durham
Johnston School

DURING THE MIDDLE Ages the border between England and Scotland was in constant turmoil and many battles were fought between the two countries. The Scots enjoyed the support of the French who were at variance with the English over their possession of lands in France. The Battle of Neville's Cross was, perhaps, one of the more important battles of the period, although it came at the culmination of a series of events.

Using his longbow archers to great advantage Edward III and his army defeated the French under Philip VI at Crécy in August 1346. They then marched triumphantly on Calais to lay siege. To try and alleviate this situation Philip asked David II of Scotland to create a diversion by mounting an invasion of northern England. By the beginning of October David had raised an army and crossed the border near Carlisle. The Scots advanced along the Tyne valley, sacked Lanercost Priory and took Hexham and neighbouring Corbridge; they drove relentlessly on and crossed the Tyne at the ford between Newburn and Ryton and continued their destructive march southwards. Legend has it that just before they crossed the River Derwent into Durham, King David had a vision warning him not to invade the lands of St Cuthbert. This warning went unheeded and the King and his army crossed the river at the old Roman Camp of Ebchester and pressed on and by 16 October they camped at Beaurepaire (Bearpark) only two miles from the cathedral city of Durham.

Meanwhile Ralph Neville, Henry Percy and the Bishop of York gathered an army at Richmond. They advanced to Barnard Castle and by the 16 October, they were camped in Auckland Park at Bishop Auckland.

Near Merrington a patrol of mounted English soldiers ran into a foraging party under the command of William Douglas. The Scots were immediately put to flight and in the following running battle many were slaughtered; this area, just to the north of Ferryhill is still known as "Butcher Race". Henry Percy sent a message to King David warning him to withdraw and return to Scotland, but this was ignored. On the night preceding the battle St Cuthbert is said to have appeared to John Fosser, the Prior of Durham, telling him to take the saint's banner into battle. It was taken to Maiden's Bower where a group of monks spent the duration of the battle in prayer.

The battle was fought on 17 October 1346. The English army of about 5000 men advanced to Crossgate Moor while the Scottish army with possibly in excess of 16 000 men advanced from Beaurepaire and drew up a little to the north. The Scots were defeated in a furious and bloody battle. The Scottish king's standard bearer, Alexander Ramsey was killed and David himself received a couple of arrow wounds. The King was captured by John Coupland who spotted his reflection as he hid under the nearby Aldin Grange bridge, however he put up a determined fight, managing to knock out Coupland's two front teeth, before being overpowered. King David was taken to Mitford Castle in Northumberland and thence to the Tower of London where he was imprisoned for 11 years before finally being ransomed for £66 000 and sum that would equate to about £25 million at today's values (about the price of a decent centre-forward!).

The Nevilles were one of the most powerful and influential families in England during the Middle Ages. After the battle Sir Ralph Neville erected a stone cross at the site to honour his great victory. Part of it can still be seen on the very spot where the English army assembled. A local story tells that if you walk three times round the cross and then put your ear to the ground you can hear the sound of the clash of arms. Sir Ralph's distinction in battle was such that he was granted the honour of being the first layman to be allowed burial in Durham Cathedral.

From then on the Banner of St Cuthbert was held in such great esteem and regarded with such deep significance by the people of the Bishopric, that the Earl of Surrey, commander of the English Army at the Battle of Flodden Field asked for it to be carried into battle by Bishop Thomas Ruthall and his army. A new sculpture was created in 1996 by Graeme Hopper and erected near the entrance of Durham Johnston School as a significant reminder of this important battle.

Neville's Cross, battle marker

Brancepeth Castle

Opposite: Brancepeth castle main gate towers

Below: Brancepeth Castle

THE HISTORY OF Brancepeth Castle dates back to pre-conquest times when it was founded by the chief of the Anglo Saxon Bulmer family whose last male heir, Bertram Bulmer, had a daughter called Emma who married Gilbert De Neuville, a Norman baron who had come to England with William the Conqueror. De Neuville's descendants became the Nevilles and owned Brancepeth Castle until the sixteenth century. However,

in 1569 Brancepeth was confiscated from the Nevilles by the Crown following the 5th Earl's involvement in the Rising of the North, the ill-fated plot to overthrow Queen Elizabeth I, restore the Roman Catholic religion, and put Mary, Queen of Scots on the throne. The Nevilles had been the chief instigators of this rising and plotted at Brancepeth and Raby Castles with the assistance of the Percys, the most powerful family in Northumberland.

Brancepeth Castle remained in the hands of the Crown for a number of years until King James I gave it to his favourite Robert Kerr (pronounced Carr), a member of the notorious Border Reiver family from Jedburgh. James made Kerr the Earl Of Somerset and also, when the lands became his, Baron Brancepeth. Unfortunately his career came to an abrupt end when he and his equally notorious wife were implicated in the poisoning and murder of Sir Thomas Overbury. From Kerr it passed to the wealthy son of a Gateshead blacksmith called Ralph Cole who also bought Kepier Hospital. However the castle was sold by his grandson, Sir Ralph, because of severe financial difficulties.

The next owner was Sir Henry Bellasis, whose daughter Mary fell in love with Bobby Shafto who lived at Whitworth Hall near Spennymoor just across the River Wear from Brancepeth. Miss Bellasis's love for Bobby became the

subject of the very famous north country song, "Bonnie Bobby Shafto" but alas Mr Shafto had eyes for someone else and Mary is said to have died of a broken heart.

In 1796 Brancepeth was bought by William Russell a Sunderland banker. The Russells of Brancepeth became one of four great coal owning families in the North called the `Grand Allies' and William's son Matthew became the richest commoner in England. Later, by marriage, Brancepeth became the property of Lord Boyne, the seventh Viscount, when he assumed the additional surname of Russell (his father-in-law's name) in 1850. In 1866, he was created Baron Brancepeth, in the Peerage of the United Kingdom. Prior to the passing of the House of Lords Act 1999, the Viscounts Boyne sat in the House of Lords in right of this title.

There have been a number of other owners since that time. The present building is largely a 19th-century restoration carried out in the 1820s by John Matthew Russell and improved in the mid-19th century by architect Anthony Salvin for William Russell, High Sheriff of Durham, in 1841.

During the First World War the castle was used as a hospital for convalescents from Newcastle General Hospital. In 1939 it became the regimental headquarters for the Durham Light Infantry, who erected a military camp of over 100 huts to the south of the village during the Second World War. The Durham Light Infantry left the Castle in 1962.

Since then it has housed a research establishment for Jobling Glassware from Sunderland, manufacturers of the famous "Pyrex".

The castle was purchased by a private owner in 1978 and is open for a couple of craft fairs and various other events several times a year.

St Brandon's Church, Brancepeth

ST BRANDON'S CHURCH, Brancepeth, is reputed to be one of only two in the country dedicated to the Celtic Saint Brandon, or Brendon, the navigator. He is said to have sailed the high seas in a leather boat in the 5th century, some historians believe he even sailed to North America. The church was originally built in the 12th century with additions in the 14th and subsequent centuries.

It was at this attractive country church that John Cosin was rector just before he was chosen as Prince Bishop of Durham at the age of 64. He was the first Prince Bishop after the Restoration and strove to repair all the ravages committed during the Commonwealth. Throughout his diocese he urged the restoration of ruined churches and chapels; he revived the church services and even rewrote the Book of Common Prayer. He became rector of St Brandon's in 1625 and he was directly responsible for the elaborate woodwork of the altar, the choir, the pews, the pulpit and font cover in the church – beautiful woodwork that was similar in style to that in Durham Cathedral.

Catastrophically a fire ravaged the church on 16 September 1998, destroying the roof, stone pillars, Victorian glass windows and much of John Cosin 's 17th century dark oak woodwork.

The long restoration project transformed the blackened interior to a bright, open spiritual place. During this project more than 100 medieval tombstones, thought to have been hidden from puritan reformers by John Cosin, were discovered in the walls. Engraved into them were mysterious symbols unique to the church, which have become known as the Brancepeth Code. Some of the best so-called cross slabs are now displayed in the church.

A new stained glass window has been installed in the chancel at the east end of the church. The Paradise Window is a modern, bold design created by designer Helen Whittaker, at Barley Studio in York and reflects St Brandon's own journey to an exotic island,

St Brandon's Church, Brancepeth

Left: St Brandon's
Church Brancepeth,
the Paradise Window

Right: St Brandon's
Church, Chancel

recorded in a book from around 900AD. It is a very original and meaningful work of art which reflects the confidence and harmony of the restored building. Keith Barley of the Barley Glass Studio comments: *"It's the sheer scale of these pieces of glass because each piece of glass has been mouth blown by a human person into a bubble which is then opened up into a sheet. I've been working with stained glass for over forty years and I've never seen a creation quite like this one."*

The Paradise Window was dedicated in a service led by the Bishop of Durham, Paul Butler on Sunday 18 May 2014.

The first recorded rector of the church was a monk from Durham called Haeming whose signature dates back to 1085. The origin of the village name has down the years been the subject of discussion, debate and argument. Some believe it relates to "Brandon's path" and refers to the route taken by St Brandon to what became known as his shrine and which today is the village church, named after him. Others prefer to believe it is associated with the "Braunspath", the braun being the wild boar that roamed freely in the area at that time and the path being the route from its lair on Brandon Hill to the River Wear. It is doubtful whether the true origin will ever be confirmed but Brancepeth Castle Golf Club has adopted the latter by displaying the boar as its club motif.

There is a legend that Brancepeth was once terrorized by an enormous brawn or boar, a dangerous beast that had made its home on Brandon Hill, and walked the forests in "ancient undisputed sovereignty". The marshy and wooded land extended from Croxdale to Ferry (*Ferie*) Wood and was among the boar's favourite haunts. Neither the Brancepeth knights or the monks of Merrington were able to get rid of this creature. But one brave knight, Roger de Ferrie, decided to do something about the creature and he carefully marked the boar's tracks, dug a pitfall, and covered it with 'boughs and turf'. To lure his victim into the pit, he used some bait and stood in the shadows of the bushes with his great sword. The fearsome beast came along his usual path, and not noticing the trap it rushed headlong towards the bait and crashed headlong into the deep pit, and Roger de Ferrie swiftly put an end to the creature with his great weapon.

According to the tradition, the bold Sir Roger is buried in the grounds of Merrington Churchyard; a coffin-shaped stone in the grounds rudely sculptured with a sword and spade on each side of the cross marks the spot.

The notorious
Brancepeth Brawn

The Ruins of Beaurepaire

Opposite: Beaurepaire – Edward I once stayed here

Below: Beaurepaire, "the Beautiful Retreat"

THE RUINS OF Beaurepaire stand on the banks of the River Browney, just to the north of the old mining village of Bearpark. The medieval estate of Beaurepaire – translated as Beautiful Retreat – was created by the Prior Bertram de Middleton (1244–1258) of Durham Cathedral when the Bishop gave permission to enclose 1300 acres of adjacent land in the mid 1200s. It suffered badly during Scottish attacks culminating in the nearby Battle of Neville's Cross in 1346. Only the shattered and roofless shell of the chapel is now standing, with dilapidated remains of some adjacent buildings.

In later centuries the building was restored and extended in by Prior John Fossor (1341–1374) to develop into a rest home for the monks of Durham. It could house up to 40 monks at any one time and the Prior continued to use it (along with his manor house at Pittington) as a favoured country residence.

Prior Hugh de Whitehead, the last Prior, is known to have carried out considerable alterations.

At the Dissolution of the Durham Priory in 1539 the estate passed to the Dean and Chapter. And the buildings continued in use as an occasional residence of the early deans of Durham,

The centre of the estate was the Prior's residence which was built in 1258 and for many years it was used as a country retreat by both the Prior of Durham and his monks. Many important guests were received here including Edward I, on his way to "hammer the Scots", Edward II, on his way home after he was hammered by the Scots, and Edward III, who was a great friend and contemporary of Bishop Thomas Hatfield. Sixteen thousand Scots under King David camped here before their defeat at the Battle of Neville's Cross on 17 October 1346.

The north wing probably contained the main hall and kitchen while the south wing housed the Prior's private apartments. The remaining ruins visible today were the large dormitory,

Today, Beaurepaire is regarded as one of the most extensive manor house sites in the North of England.

Finchale Priory

Finchale Priory – once a holiday home for the monks of Durham

FINCHALE PRIORY CAN be found in a secluded spot on a bend in the River Wear about four miles from the centre of Durham. The steep river banks and the overhanging trees do their best to hide the ruin from view.

Finchale Priory – once a holiday home for the monks of Durham

Some historians believe that this is where Ethelwald, King of Northumbria died in 765AD. it is also thought hat a synod was held here in 792AD by Higbald, Bishop Of Lindisfarne, for the regulation of church discipline. It can't have worked because this synod was followed in 798 and in 810 by others for the same purpose.

However, Finchale is probably best known for its association with St Godric who made his home here in the 12th century. Godric was born in Walpole in Norfolk in 1065 and for the early part of his adult life was a successful pedlar. Later he became part owner of a coasting vessel and made his living as a sea trader and part time pirate if the stories are to be believed.

On one of his voyages he visited Lindisfarne where the story of St Cuthbert had a profound effect on him and he forthwith made a pilgrimage to Jerusalem. He made a further pilgrimage to Rome accompanied by his mother. Godric eventually settled in Weardale as a disciple of the hermit Alric, who is reputed to have shared his cave with a pack of savage wolves. After two years Alric died, although there is no record of him being eaten by wolves, and Godric made a further pilgrimage to the Holy Land.

On his return he first settled in Whitby but eventually travelled to Durham where he became sacrist at St Giles' Church. It was here that he learned to read and write, however his desire to became a hermit was overwhelming and he obtained permission from Bishop Flambard to settle in a "snake-infested" spot near Finchale.

He built himself a hut and a small oratory which he dedicated to St Mary. It was a bit of a strange hermitage because his mother, brother and sister

Finchale Priory – the steps from the nave

Finchale Priory - the cross allegedly marks the burial place of St Godric

followed him to Finchale. His mother died shortly afterwards and his brother was drowned in the River Wear, but his sister lived nearby for many years.

When he moved to Finchale, Godric observed all the austerities of a hermit. He used a stone for a pillow and would only eat food when it was rotten. His daily bread was made half of flour and half of ashes. He dug a small bath in the stony ground near the river and often stood naked, up to his neck in freezing cold water, praying throughout the night.

The deadly poisonous snakes didn't bother him and, indeed, they came into his hut and even entwined themselves round his legs to keep warm in the cold winter.

He was robbed and almost killed by a pack of invading Scots in 1138 and his home was nearly washed away in a great flood in 1149. In his gratitude for it being saved he built a bigger oratory which he had dedicated to St John the Baptist by Bishop William de St Barbara.

Every Sunday and holy day a monk would travel from Durham to celebrate mass in his oratory. But for the last few years of his life Godric was confined to his bed and lived only on milk. He died on 21 May 1170, at the age of 105, and was buried in his oratory.

Finchale then became the residence of two monks, Henry and Reginald, who wrote his biography.

In 1241 the Archbishop of York ordered a new church to be built at Finchale with five resident monks. It became a "holiday home" for the monks of Durham who visited on a rota system, four at a time to join the five resident monks. Discipline seems to have been a little slack here because the monks were severely reprimanded for keeping a pack of hounds and wearing linen shirts in preference to their monks' habits.

In the general upheaval that came with the Dissolution Godric's body vanished, but the site of his empty tomb is marked by a stone cross set into the floor of the nave.

Finchale Priory is now in the care of English Heritage and is possibly one of Durham's most interesting monastic ruins.

Finchale Priory from across the River Wear

The mysterious
undercroft, Finchale
Priory

Ludworth Tower

LUDWORTH TOWER STANDS at the very edge of Durham City's eastern boundary.

In 1411 the manor of Ludworth passed into the hands of the Holden family who built the original dwelling. In 1422 a Palatinate licence was granted to Thomas Holden to enclose, fortify and crenellate his manor house by Cardinal Thomas Langley, Bishop of Durham. Only a few vestiges of the tower now stand. Over the remains of a tunnel-vaulted basement are two fragments of the three-storey west wall, with various window openings, the openings of fireplaces and a first floor spiral staircase. The south and east walls collapsed in the late 19th century and are now grass covered banks and foundation remains. The peel tower was once encased by a rectangular bank and ditch. The surrounding village was largely deserted by the late 15th century.

Ludworth Tower; its scant remains can be seen for miles

Opposite: Ludworth Tower a strongly fortified tower house

133

St Laurence Church, Pittington

ST LAURENCE CHURCH, Pittington is a hidden gem, absolutely beautiful in both architecture and decoration. It is possible that Christians have worshipped here since 1100AD, and furthermore it is thought to have been built on the site of an earlier wooden church. A settlement has existed here from early times; and it is quite possible that St Aidan visited here whilst on his extensive travels throughout Northumbria.

The Venerable Bede records that the Pope sent relics of St Laurence, who was one of the seven deacons of ancient Rome who were martyred during the persecution of Emperor Valerian in 258, to Oswy, King of Northumbria in 667AD and this may suggest that an earlier church was founded here at that time.

Opposite: St Laurence Church, Pittington, in winter

Below: 12th century wall paintings of St Cuthbert

One of the treasures of the church is a set of two 12th century paintings depicting scenes from the life of St Cuthbert; they can be found in the splays of a window at the western end of the church. It is widely believed that much of the church interior was decorated in this manner but sadly only these two examples survive. In the centre of this beautifully decorated arch, above the aperture, is some very elaborate foliated scrollwork which may be intended to symbolise vines – it bears more than a passing resemblance to similar work in the Galilee Chapel in Durham Cathedral – it is this kind of beautifully flowing detail that is typical of very high quality early decorative work. The scene in the left hand splay of the window depicts Cuthbert at his consecration as bishop – he is the tonsured figure kneeling on the left, having the holy oil poured over his head by Archbishop Theodore. It is thought that the crowned man at the far right of the scene could possibly be King Egfrith of Northumbria, who was also present at the consecration in York.

The painting of the figures can also be compared to that of St Cuthbert in the Galilee Chapel in Durham Cathedral – the similarities are so great that it seems in all probability both were done by the same artist.

The painting in the right hand splay of the window is a unique depiction of St. Cuthbert's vision at the table of Abbess Aelfled of Whitby, a close friend whom he visited more than once. Cuthbert, by this time had become Bishop of Lindisfarne, and was invited by Aelfled to visit her at her monastery and share a meal. The painting shows the moment that when eating at Aelfled's table, he dropped his knife at the moment he experienced a vision of 'the soul of a holy man' being taken to Heaven. There is more scrollwork at the top of this painting, and below that the holy man's soul painted as a small figure lying horizontally across the space, head at the right, legs in the air and one hand extended downwards. Bede's story tells how the vision was confirmed when a messenger brought news that one of Aelfled's servants had fallen to his death from a tree.

This messenger is the young man in a light brown tunic at the far right of the scene, his hand on the table, speaking to Aelfled, who is wearing a green veil around her head and raises her right hand from the table in shock. A tall man, also in brown, stands behind, and then comes Cuthbert in a red cloak, his left hand gripping the edge of the table as the truth of his vision is confirmed. The table is set with a fish on a dish, a cup for wine or other drink, and bread.

Hanging at the west end of the south aisle are two framed full-scale reproductions of the 12th-century wall paintings with accompanying text stating that they were done by Mr N. Hamlyn of Bishop Hatfield's Hall, Durham, in around 1888.

About 1180, during the episcopate of Bishop Pudsey (Hugh de Puiset) the church was extended considerably. An aisle was added to the original north wall, this was then pierced and the decorated pillars and arches were added. The first four arches date from this period, as does the large arch on the west wall and the lower part of the tower. The similarity with 12th century building in Durham Cathedral is again apparent. Bishop Pudsey was responsible for the Galilee Chapel in Durham Cathedral and the Norman Gallery in Durham Castle. He had two great builders: Ricardus the Ingenator (a name from which the modern word engineer is derived) who was known as Pudsey's architect, and Christian the Mason. They both held lands in Sherburn and Pittington, and almost certainly lived in the area. Christian's grave cover is a massive slab of Frosterley marble sited near the pulpit. Some historians believe he was responsible for both the Galilee Chapel in Durham and the north arcade in St Laurence.

St Laurence – drawings of the wall paintings reproduced in 1888

Opposite: St Laurence Church interior shows a passing resemblance to Durham Cathedral

Croxdale Hall, Norman Church and Sunderland Bridge

SUNDERLAND BRIDGE ORIGINALLY carried the Great North Road (A1) across the River Wear, and probably dates back to the 14th century. It is a Grade I listed structure. It is built of dressed sandstone with four semicircular arches. The bridge has undergone several rebuilds, with the end arches being rebuilt after the Great Flood in 1770, the parapets widened in 1822, and new end walls built in the 19th century. The bridge is quite narrow and measures only 18 feet between the parapets. However it is generally thought

Croxdale Norman Church

to be one of the most attractive bridges on the River Wear. In 1924 Durham County Council built the new Croxdale Bridge just to the east, to carry the A1 main road because the existing bridge couldn't handle the increasing amount of traffic. The A1 was later re-designated the A167, and Croxdale Bridge continues to carry this road.

The half mile walk from Sunderland Bridge through parkland to Croxdale Hall is an easy and rewarding exercise. The Norman church behind the Hall is an unexpected bonus.

Due to the deterioration to the interior it is presently only possible to view the church over the churchyard wall. There is, however, much to note, not least the Norman doorway with its apparently original door complete with ornate iron hinge strapwork. In the tympanum the carving is now heavily weathered but is still discernible as a representation of the tree of life.

Originally built as one of four chapels of ease to St Oswald's parish in Durham, it was inherited by the Catholic Salvin family when they came to Croxdale in 1402. They built the present Croxdale hall around 1760. In 1807 they added a substantial chapel in Gothic style integral with the hall and almost opposite the small church.

Croxdale Norman Church,
from the north-east

In 1845 when the Dean and Chapter sought land to build a larger and more conveniently located church the Salvins provided the present site of St Bartholomew's in Sunderland Bridge village and received the old church in exchange, which then, unfortunately, fell into disuse, the churchyard being used only for family burials. More recently however, the fabric of the church has been greatly restored and is a Grade I listed building.

The privately owned, Grade I listed, Croxdale Hall can be seen from the nearby footpath. It originally came into the staunchly Roman Catholic Salvin family through the marriage in 1402 of Gerard Salvin of Harswell, Yorkshire to Agnes Wharton, heiress of Croxdale. They have held the property ever since. The house was originally in the Tudor style and dates from the 17th century but major alterations in about 1760 were carried out probably to designs by architect John Carr, including the two storey seven-bay west entrance front.

Croxdale Hall from the public footpath

The impressive internal Rococo plasterwork dates from this time. Further alterations were carried out by architect James Wyatt in about 1807 including the addition of a five-bay south wing and the insertion of a Gothic Revival-style Roman Catholic chapel into the 18th century north wing.

The house served as a military hospital 1940–1945 and thereafter as a maternity home until at least 1954. More recently the Hall has been restored as a family home.

Old Croxdale Bridge
an excellent example
of a coaching bridge

Langley Hall, a Fortified Manor House

HIDDEN IN DENSE woodland, just to the west of Witton Gilbert, right on the western border of Durham City are the remains of Langley Hall, a fortified manor house. Langley was in the hands of the Scrope (pronounced Scroop) family from the 14th century until the direct line of the family came to an end with the death of Emanuel Lord Scrope in 1630.

It is generally thought that the Hall was built by Henry Lord Scrope who died in 1533. Durham historian Hutchinson records that his name is carved over the Hall fireplace.

In the 17th century it passed to the family of the Marquis of Winchester and then in the 18th century to the Lambtons, by which time the buildings had fallen into ruin, and were being used as a farm. The remains have continued to deteriorate throughout the 19th and 20th centuries, considerable sections of wall having fallen within the last 40 or 50 years. Part of the hall was turned into a farmhouse which was still in use in 1835. The ruins comprise the remains of two ranges of buildings set on the opposite sides of a courtyard about sixty feet square. What's left of the building is in a dangerously ruinous condition despite standing to a height of three storeys on the west wing. However the gaunt shell provides ample evidence of the original layout and construction. Thus the

Langley Hall a spooky ruin in dense woodland

A tantalising glimpse of Langley hall from the neighbouring footpath.

standing remains are almost entirely of the west and east ranges; there has clearly been a north range and probably also one on the south, although its exact position is no longer clear.

The ruins stand inside the roughly rectangular remains of a moat. This is best preserved on the north, and still holds water around the north-west corner. The south-east angle of the enclosure is cut across by a track that forms the boundary of the present woodland.

These spooky ruins also have a ghost story linked with them. During the waning gibbous moon it is said that a black coach, containing a black coffin, pulled by four black headless horses driven by a headless driver in a black cloak, thunders down the old overgrown track from Old Hall Wood to Langley Lane. And they can't see where they are going!